Void

GADFLY

First published 2020
Gadfly Editions

British Library Cataloguing in Publication Data
A CIP catalogue record for this book is
available from the British Library

ISBN 978-0-9928060-7-1 Casebound

Photography, artwork, design
and typesetting by Martyn Clark
Adobe Garamond Pro 11pt.

**www.gadflyeditions.com
www.martynclark.com**

For Luarda, and
the people I have
loved and lost.

Void

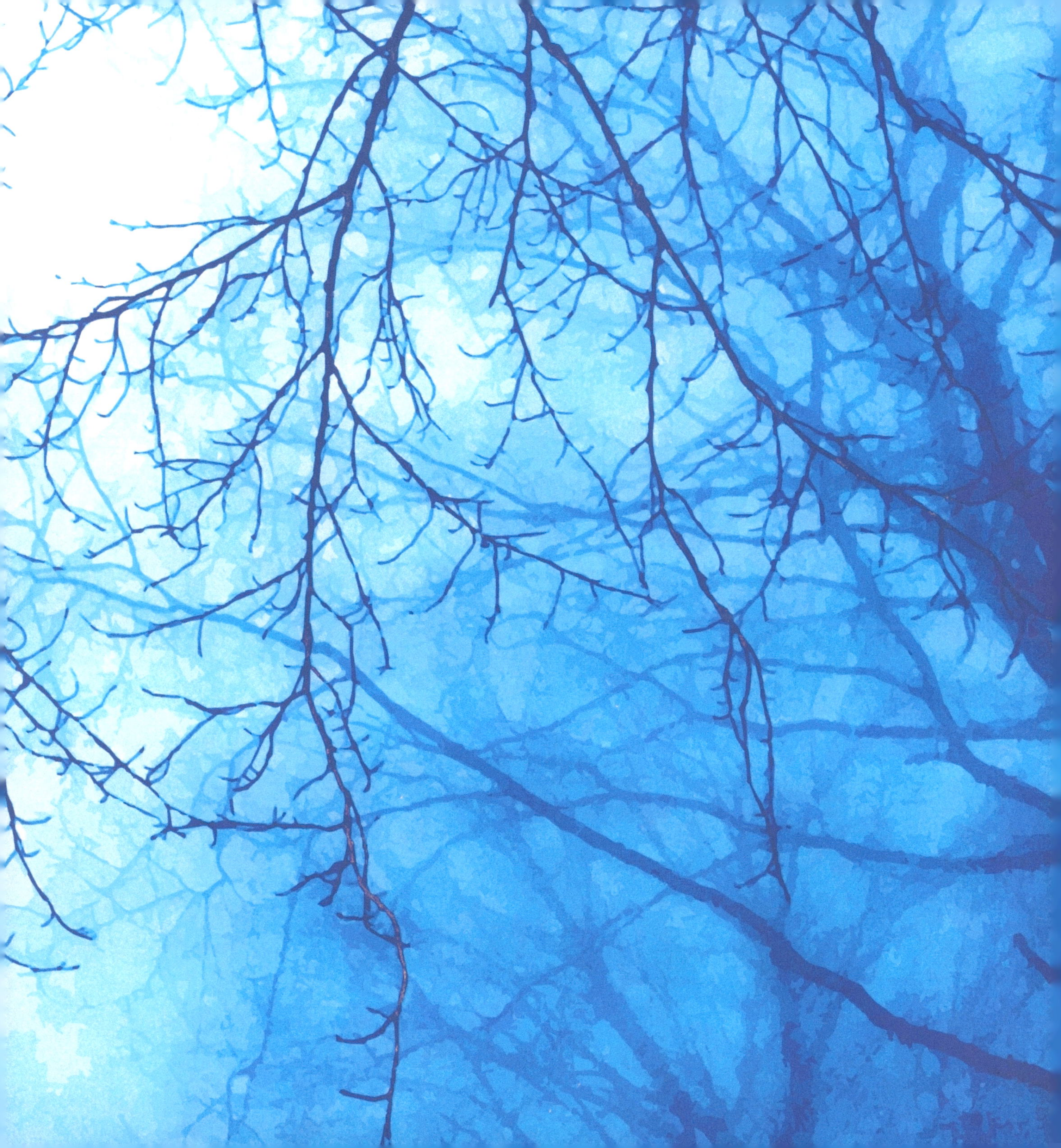

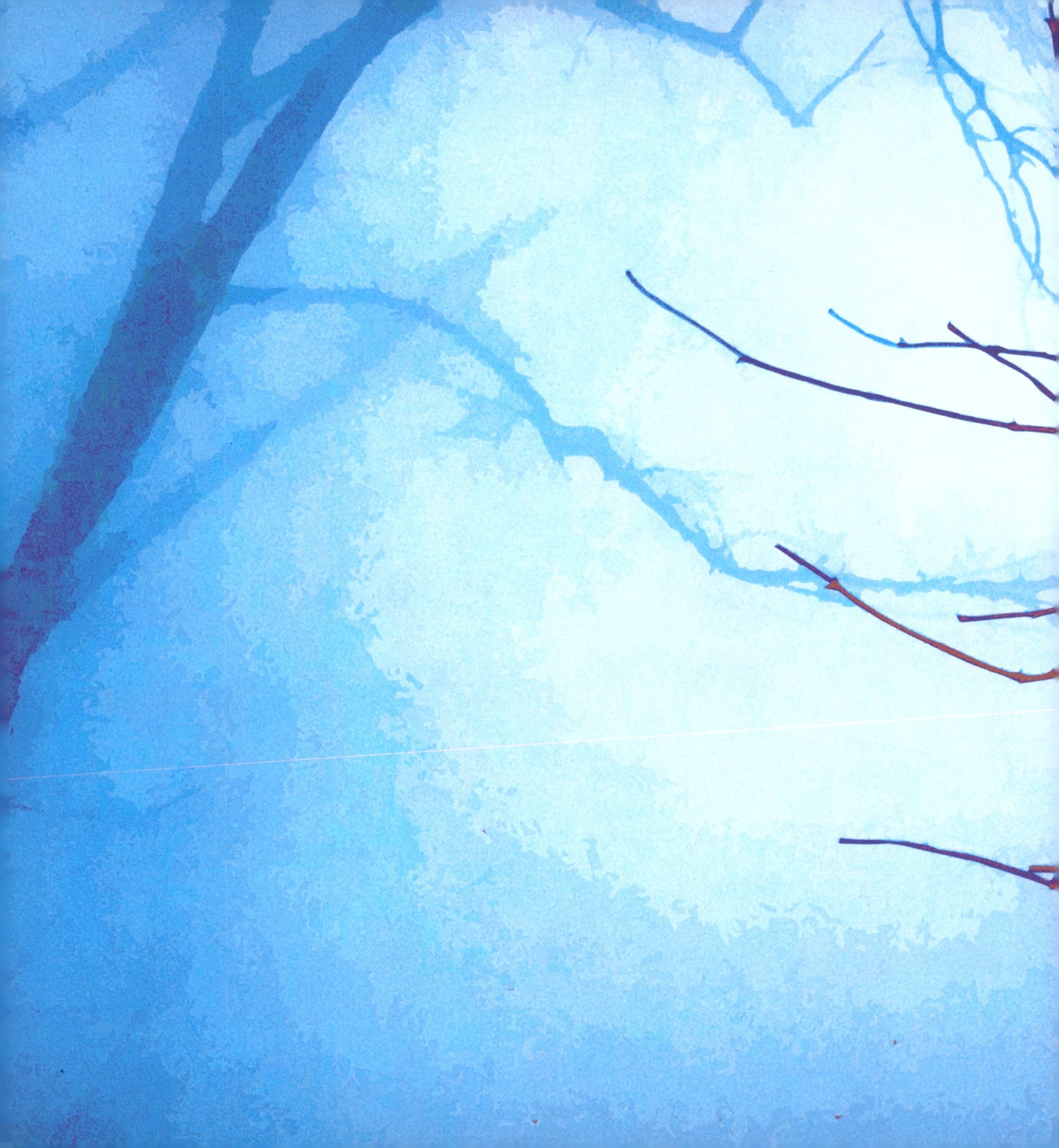

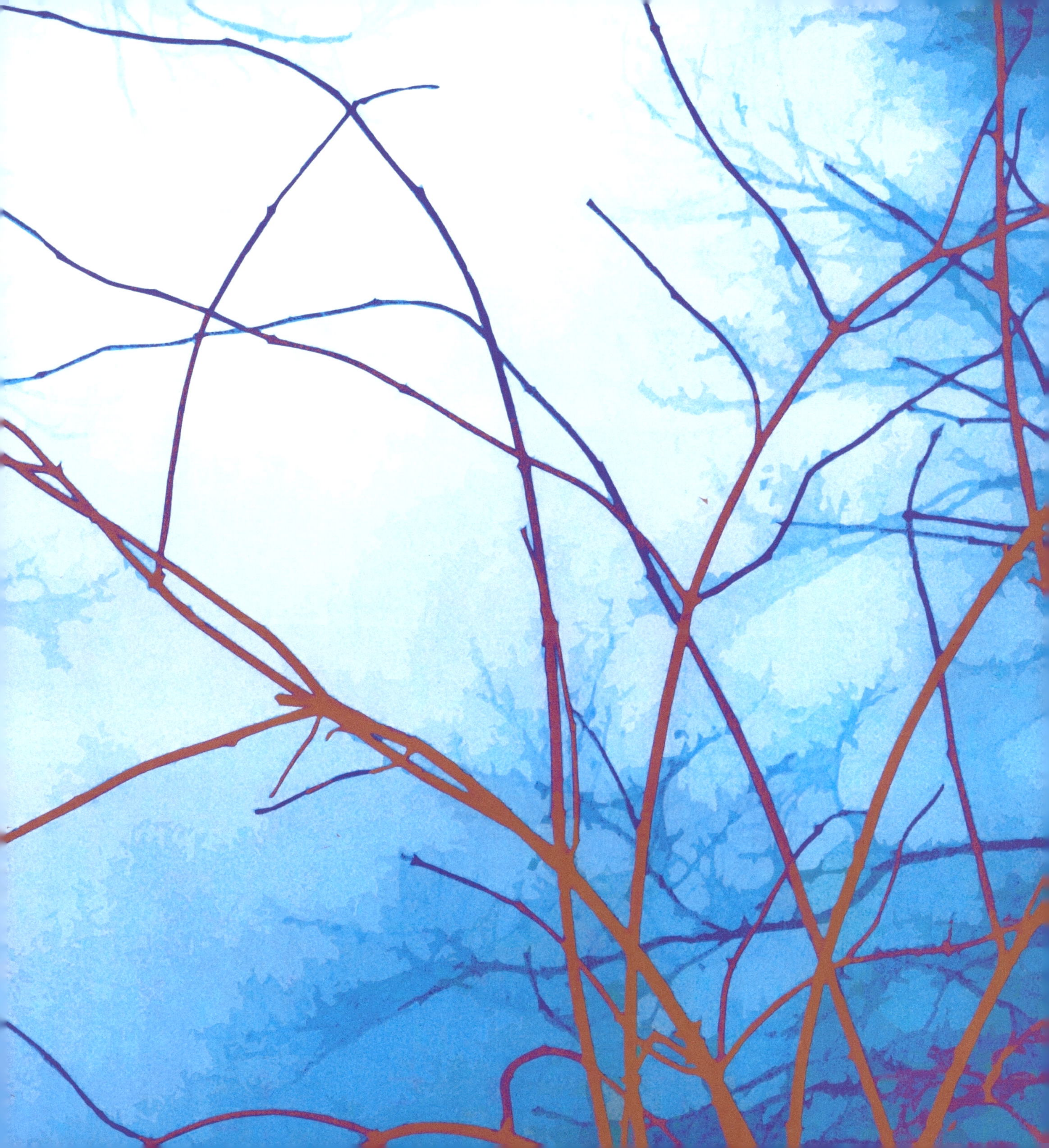

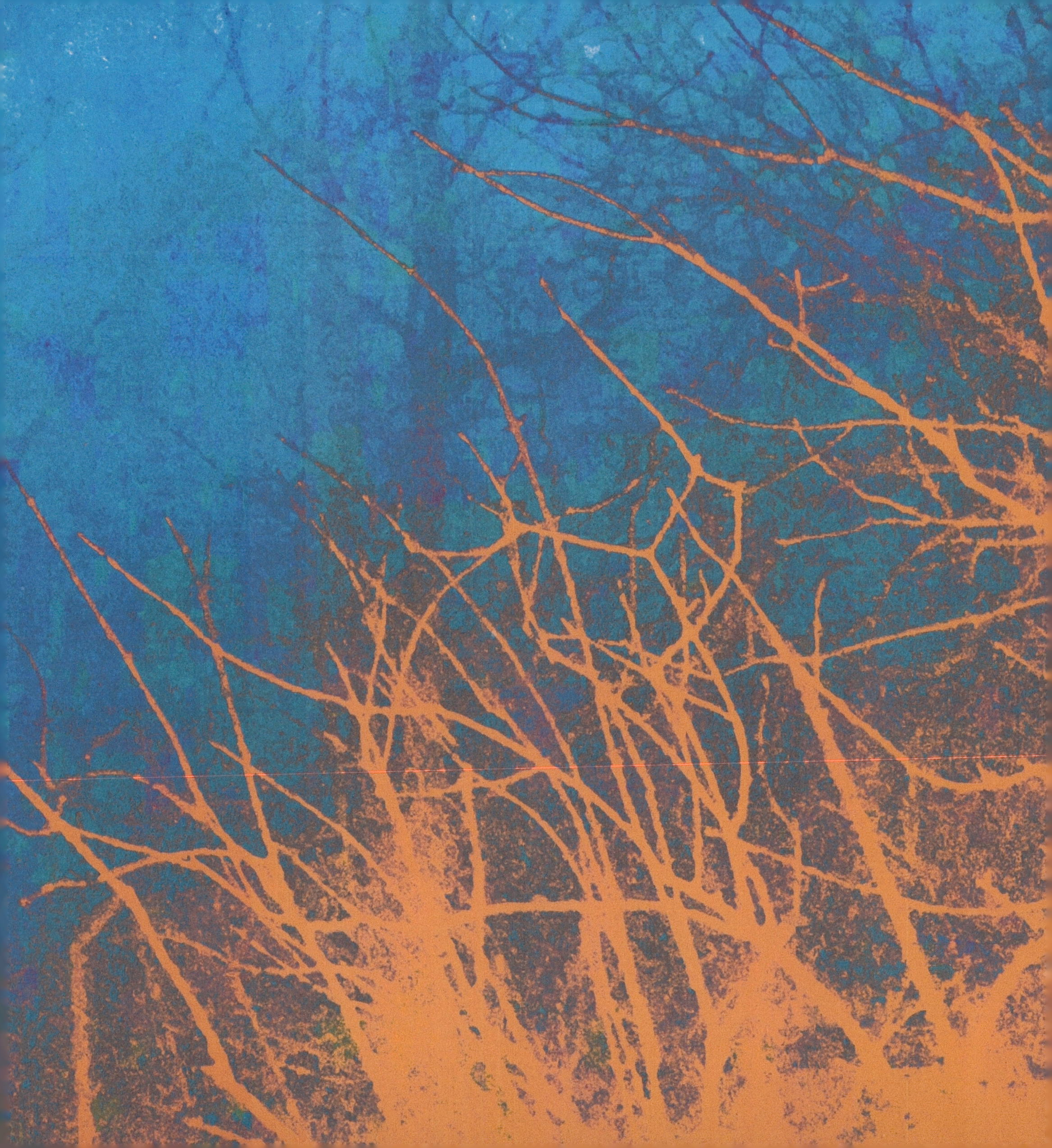

At the end of the world,
we will see our dreams come true.

There's always hope,
they say—

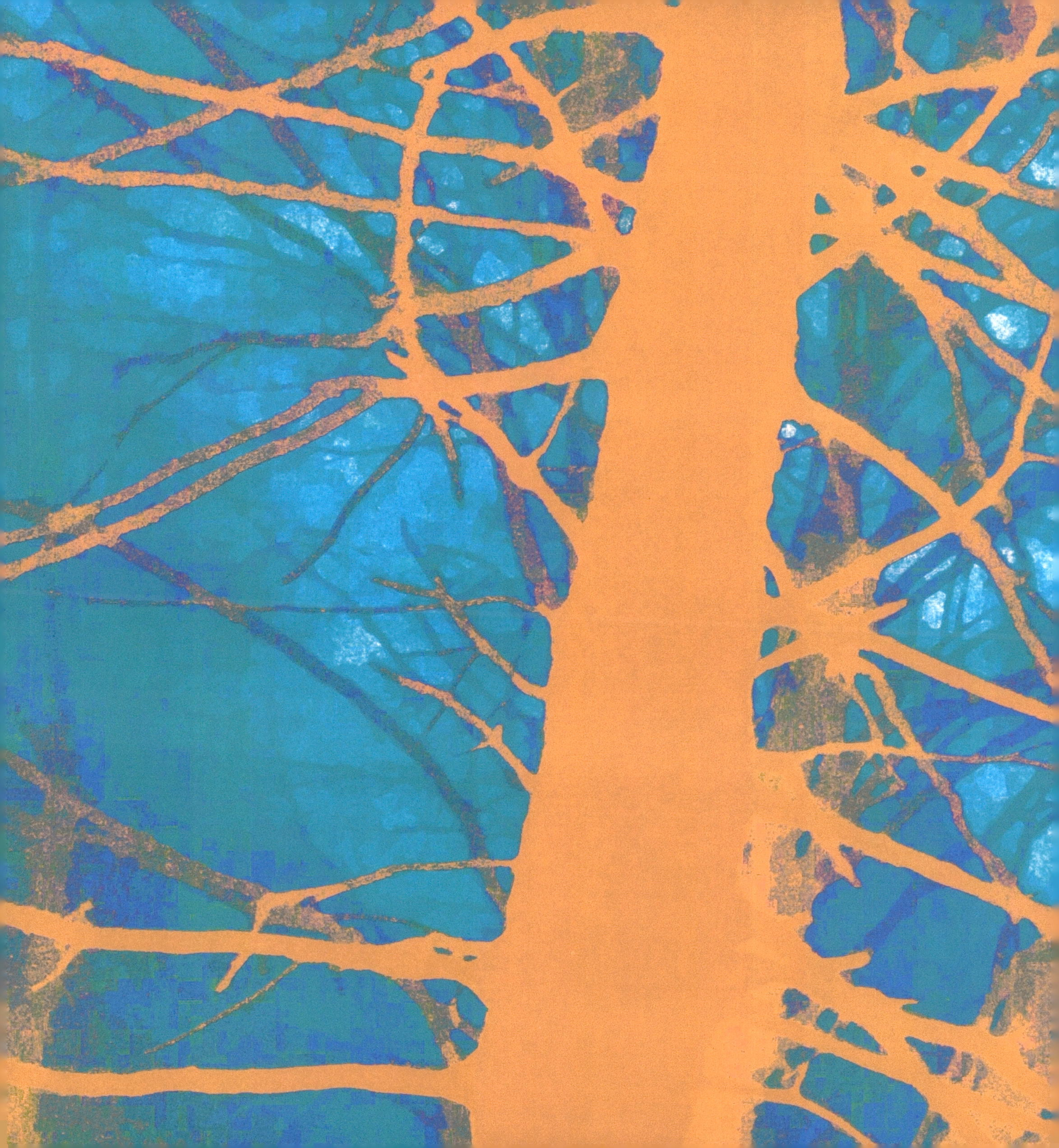

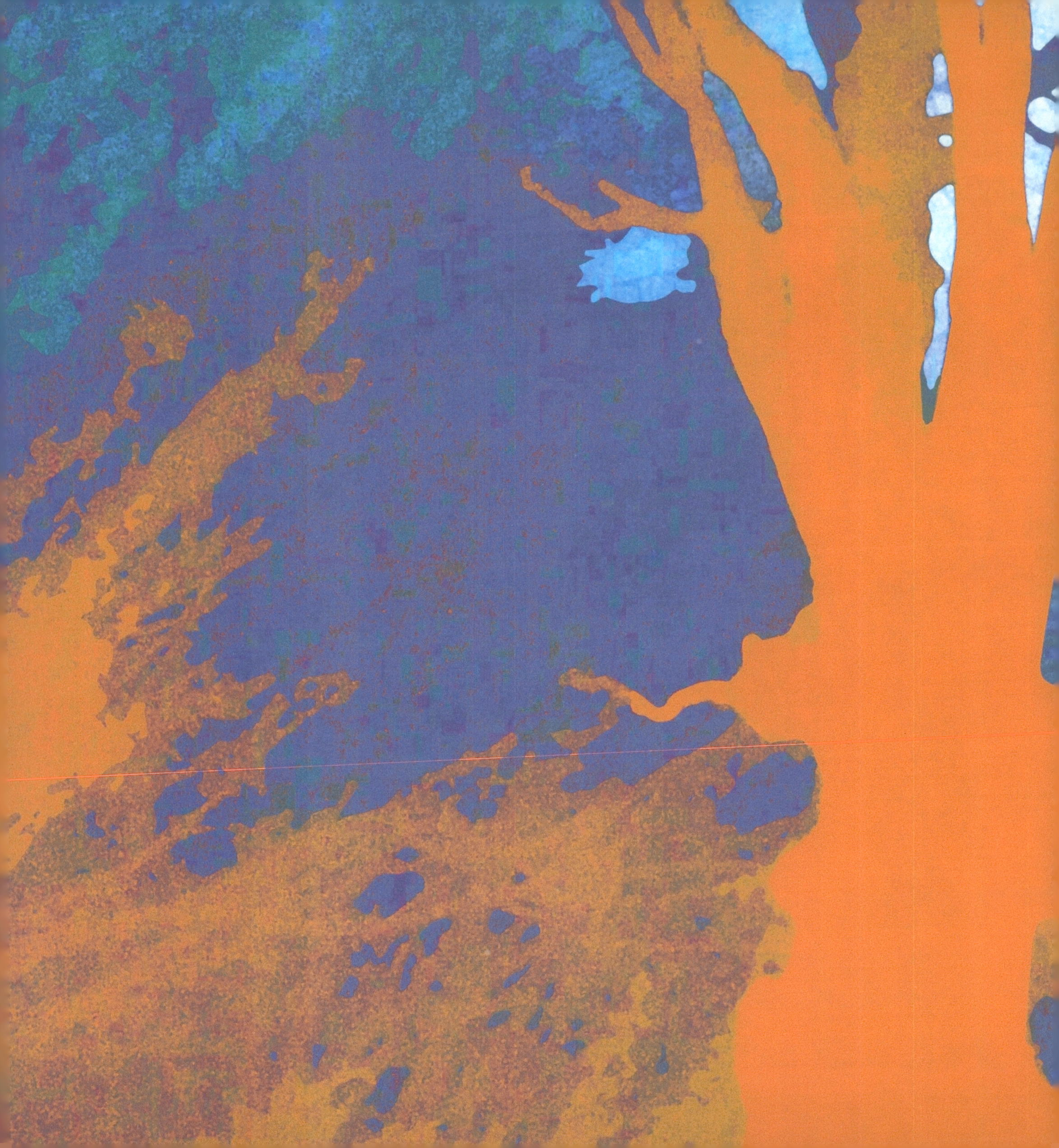

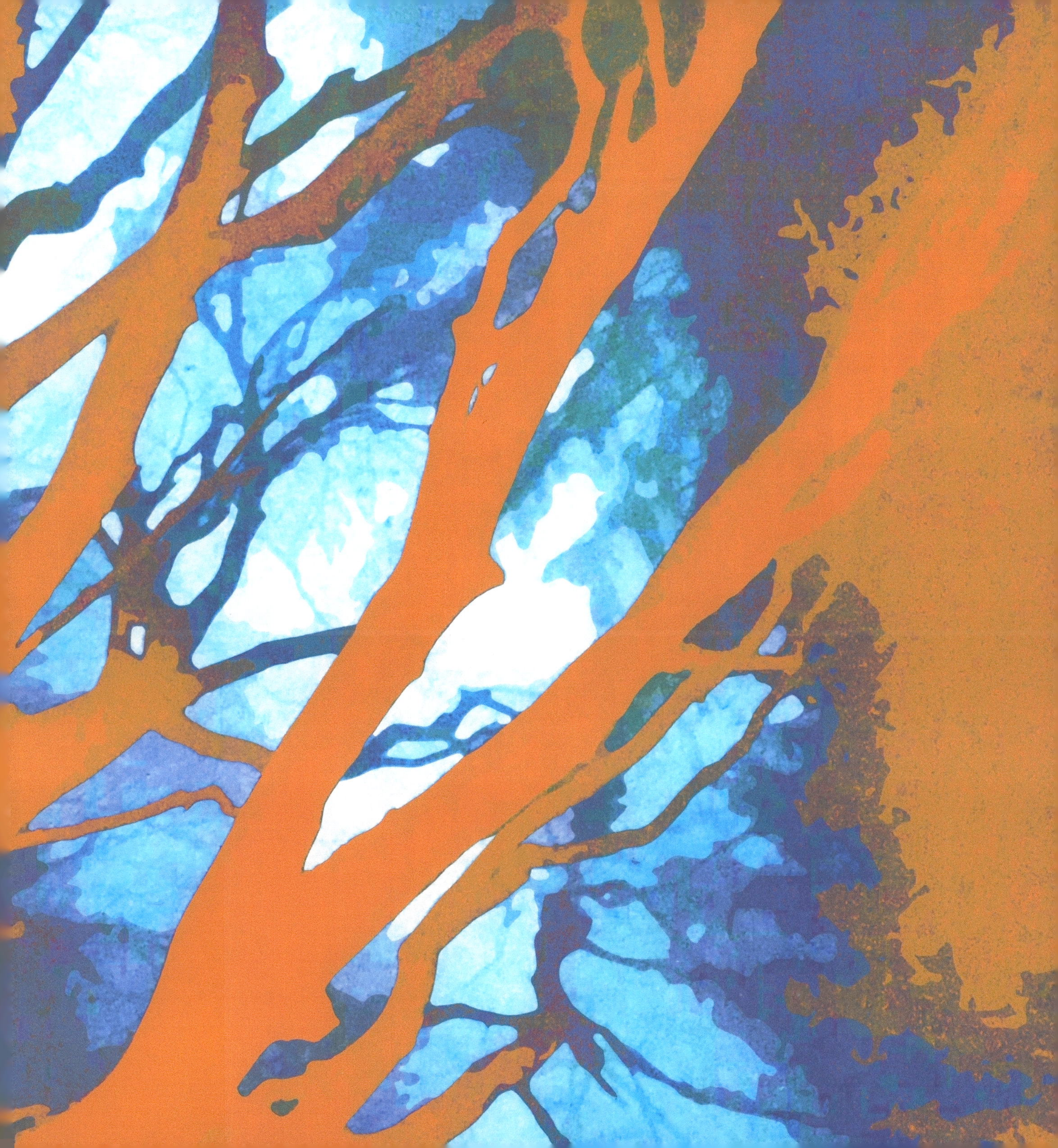

Build something beautiful
around your void.

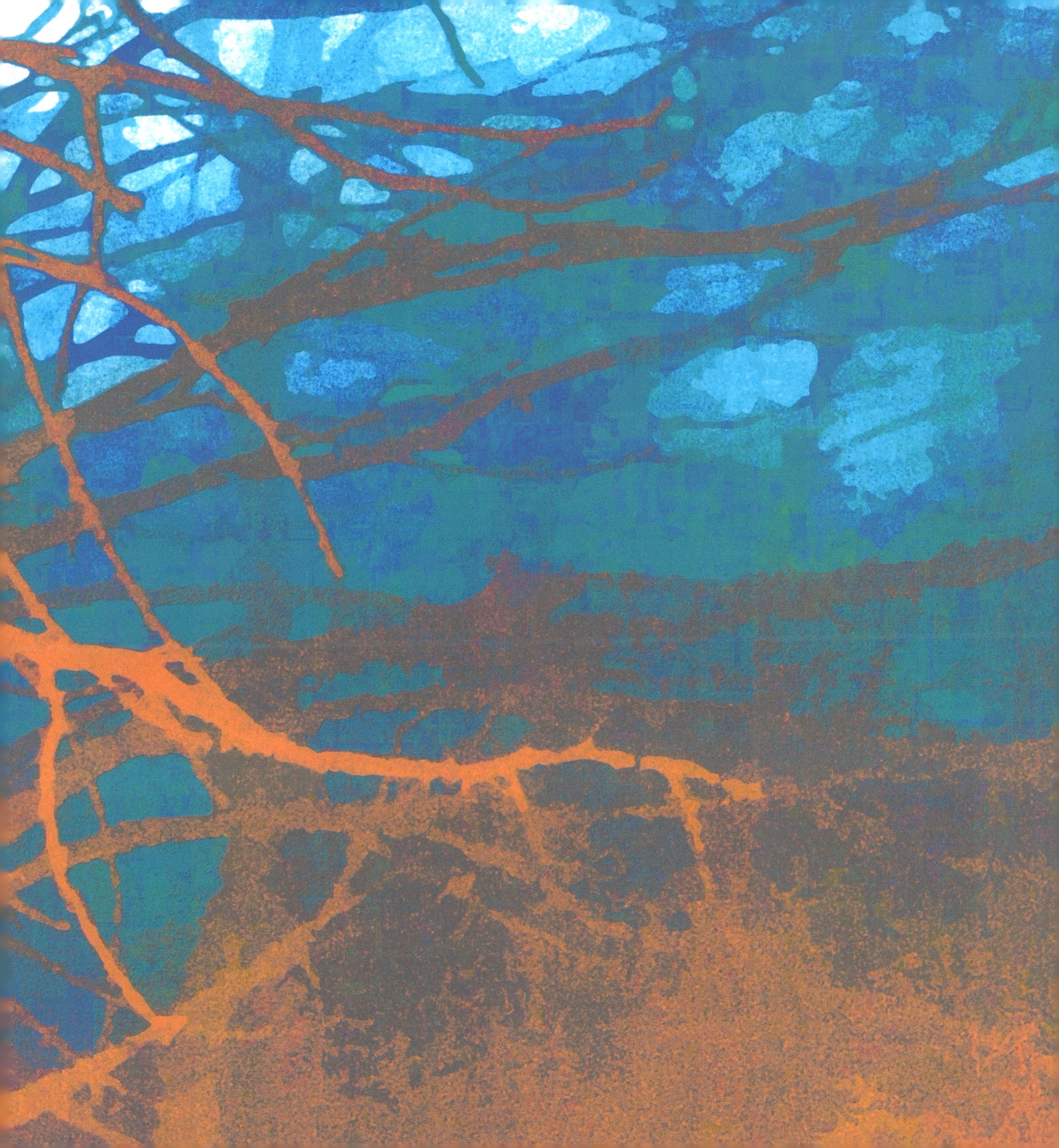

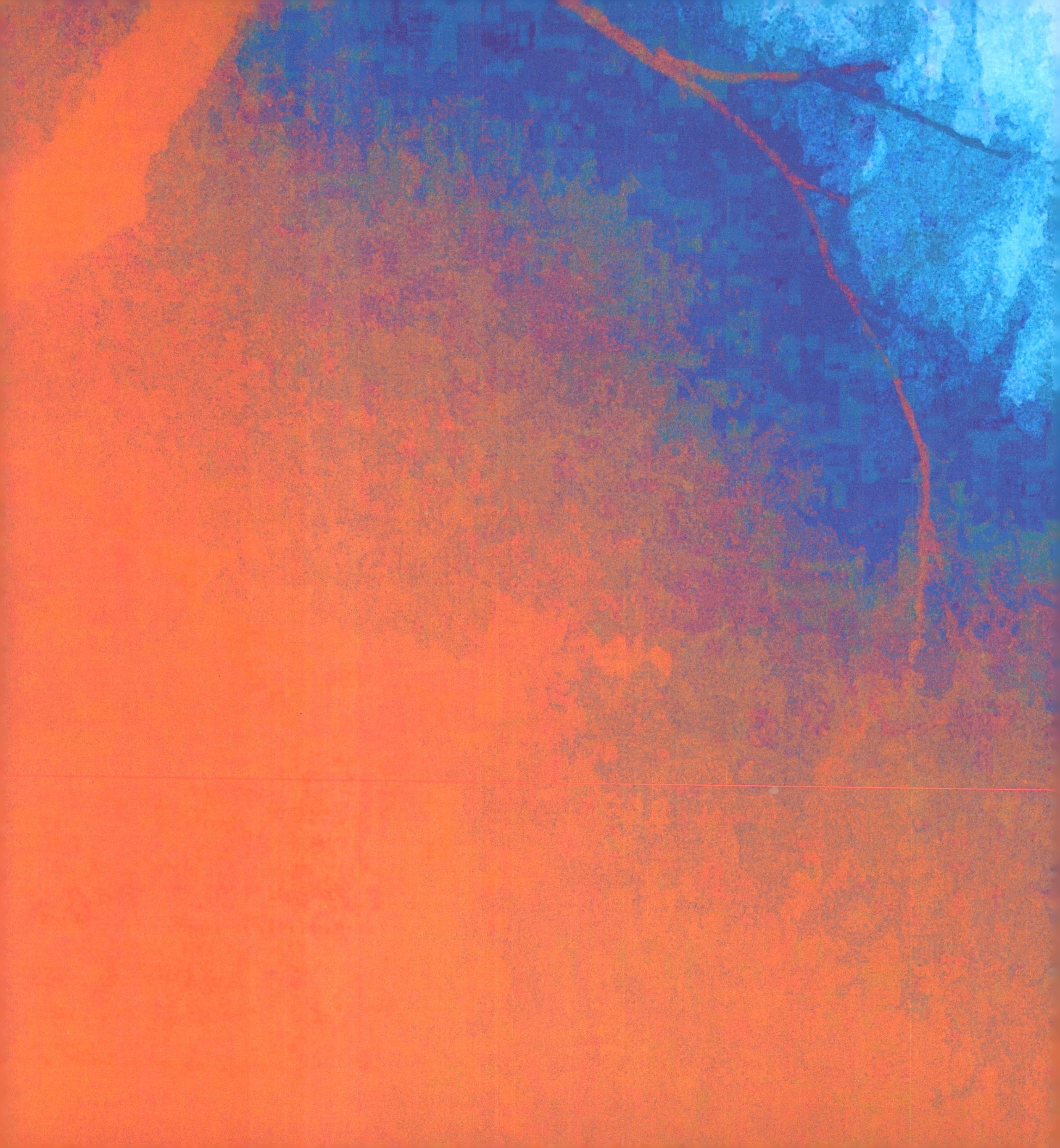

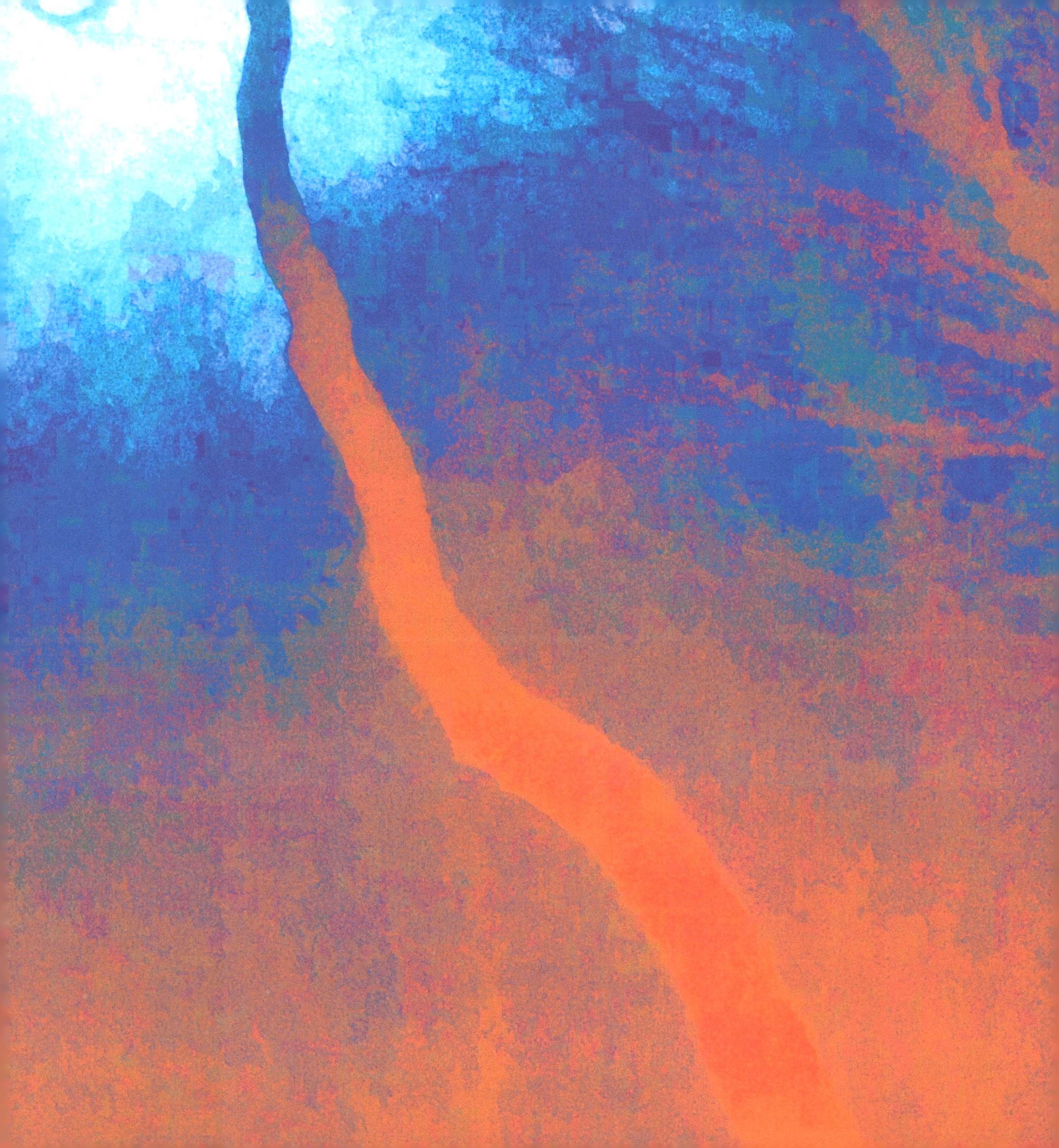

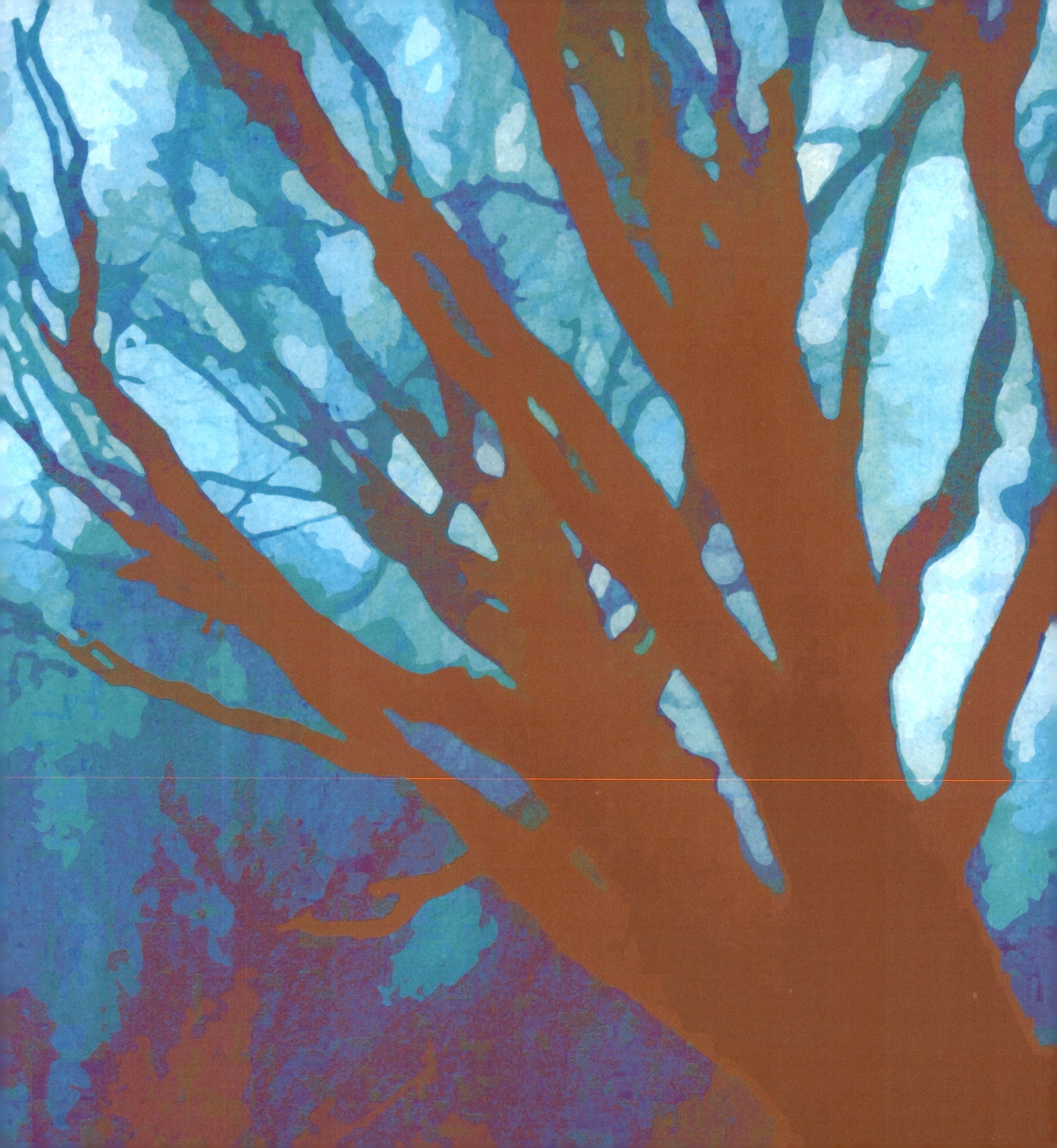

But the void
is the beauty—

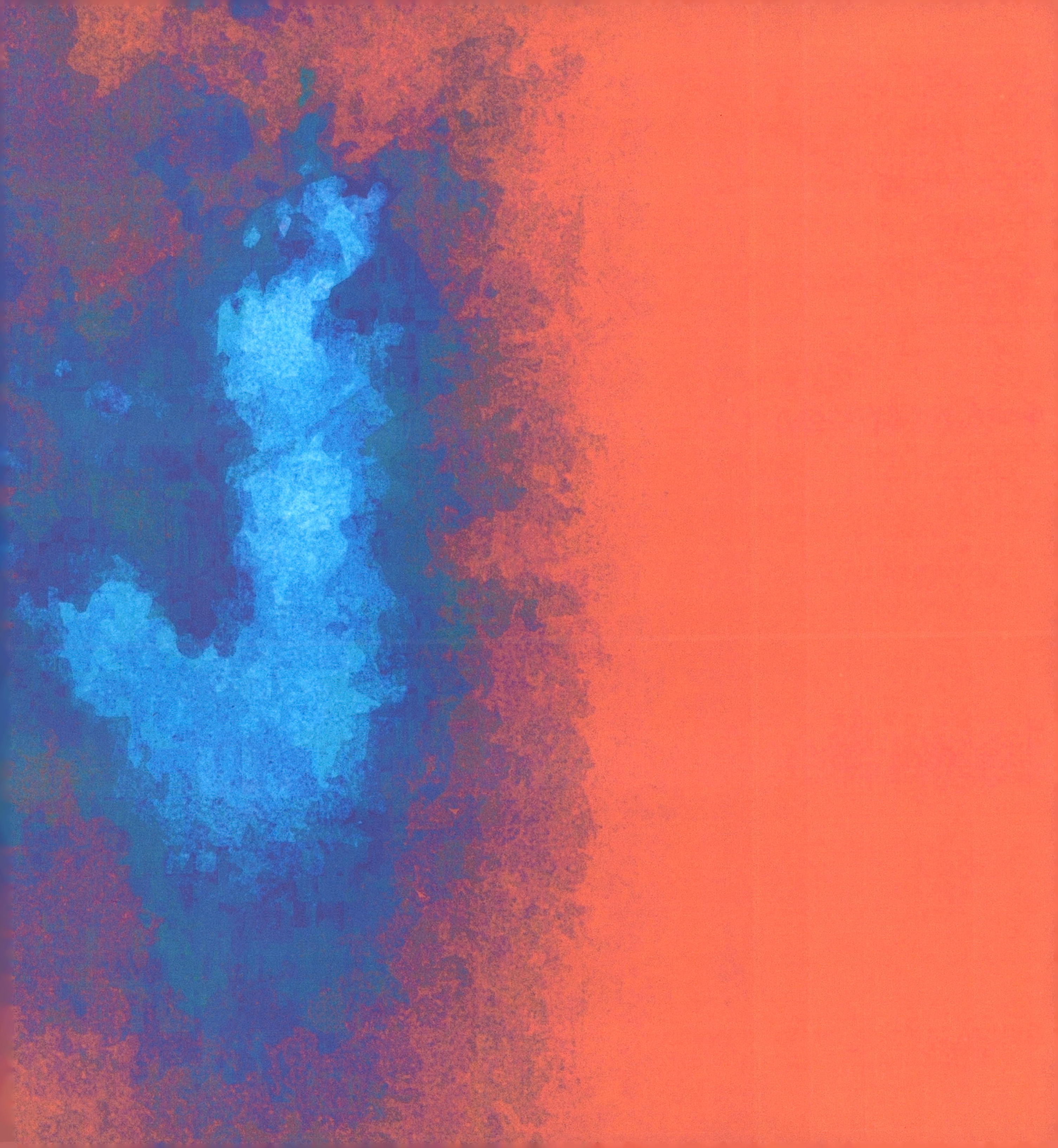

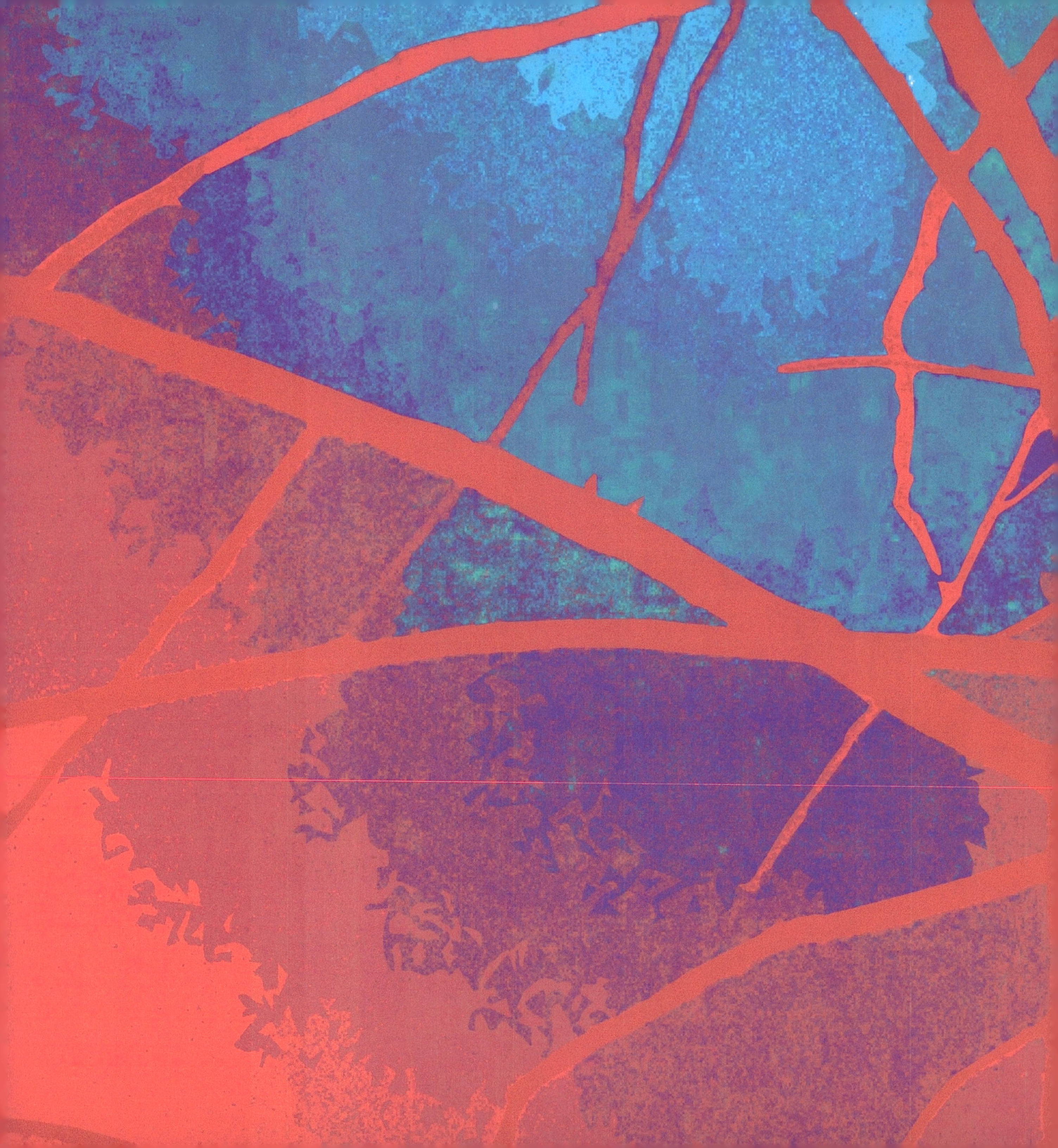

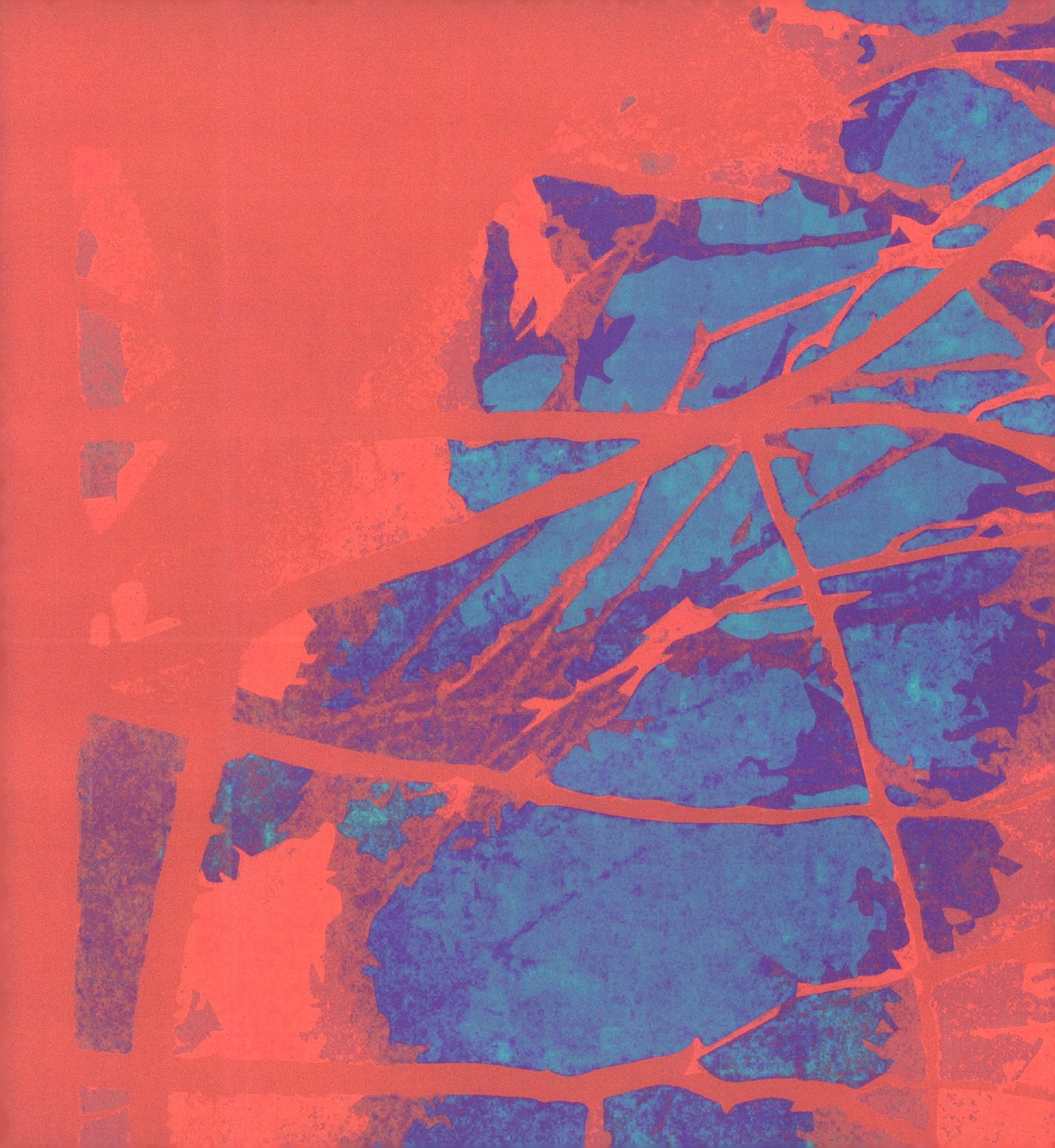

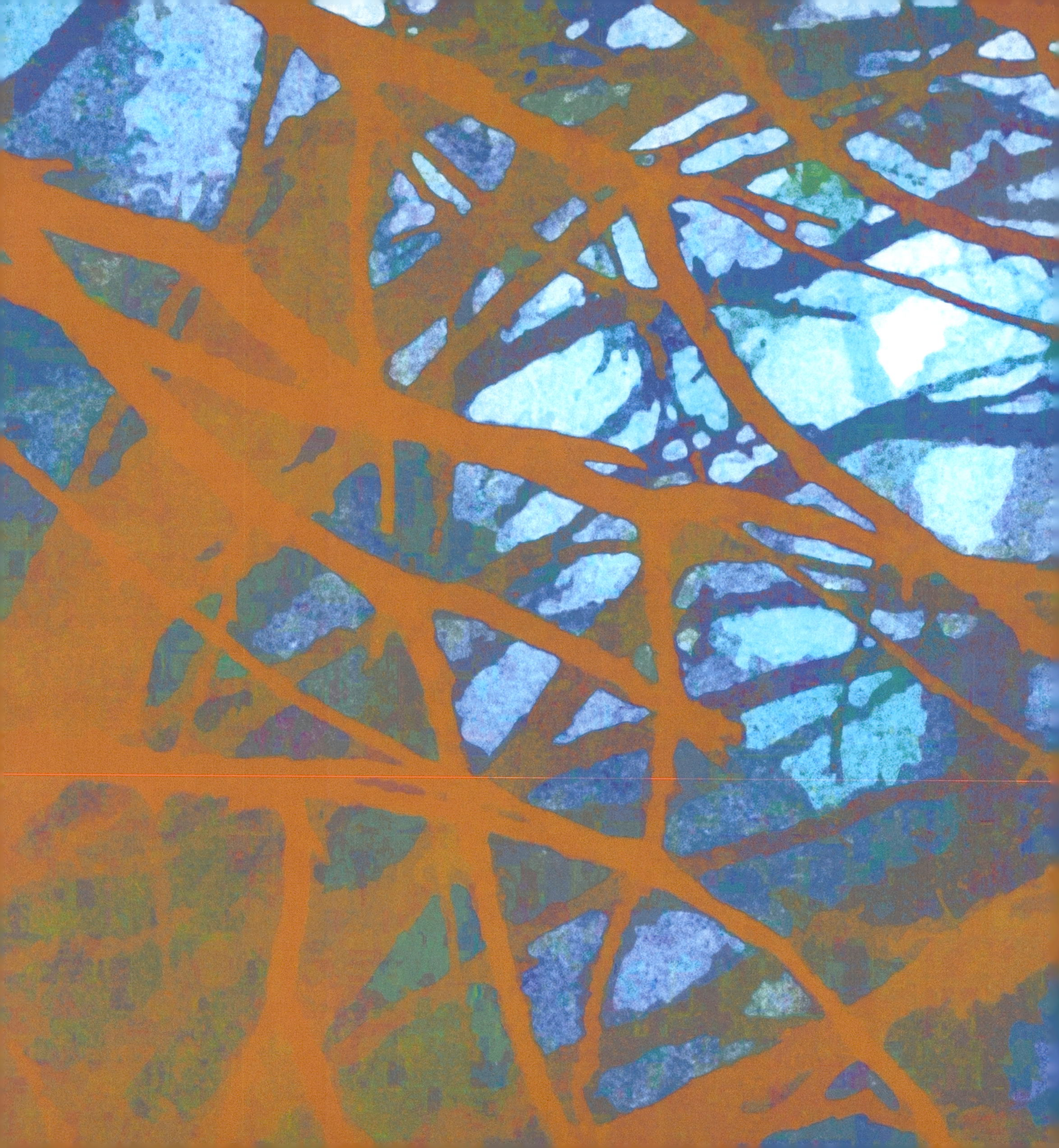

Love without end,
that comes and goes.

Signs of it, everywhere,
at the bottom of my soul.

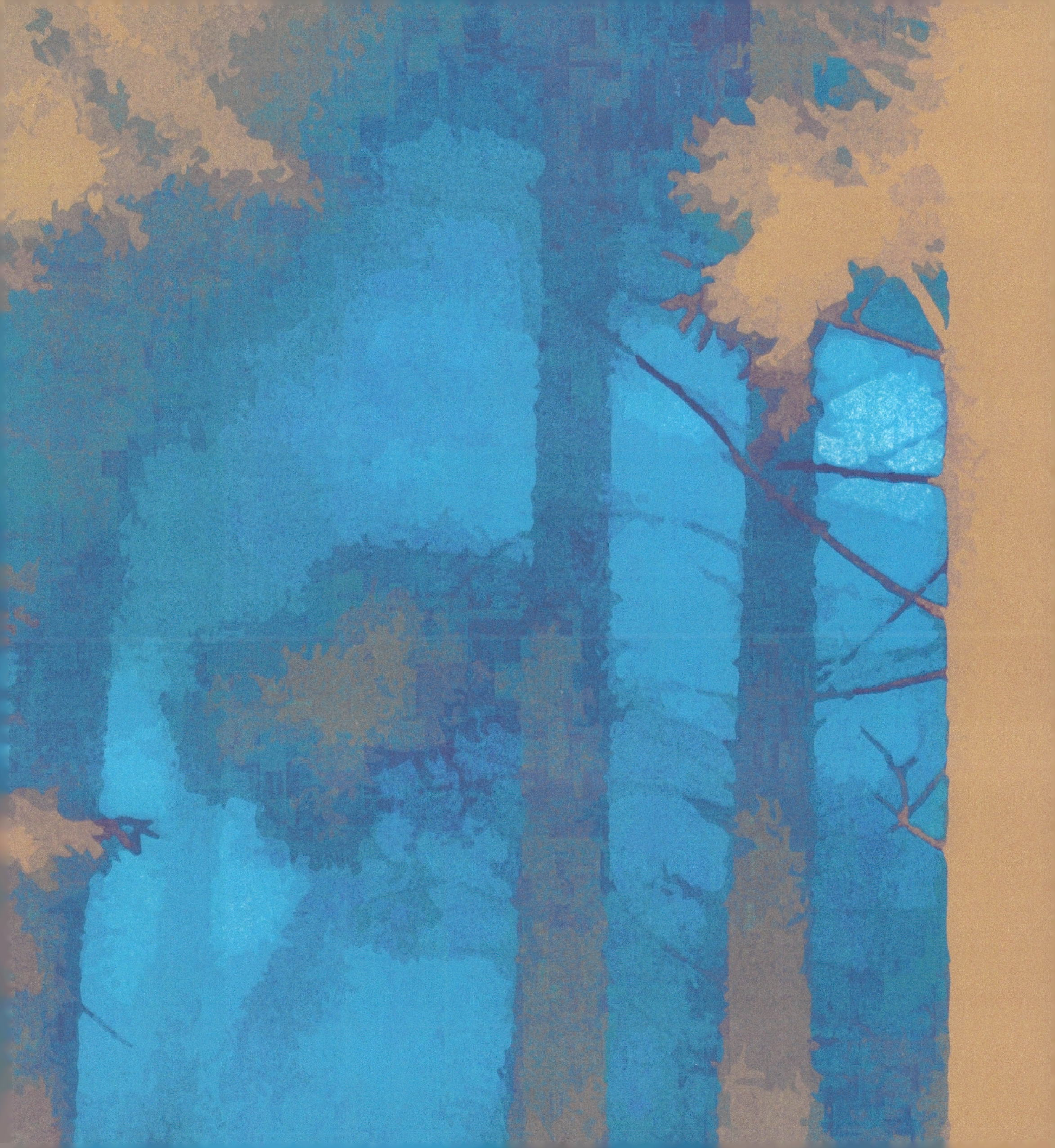

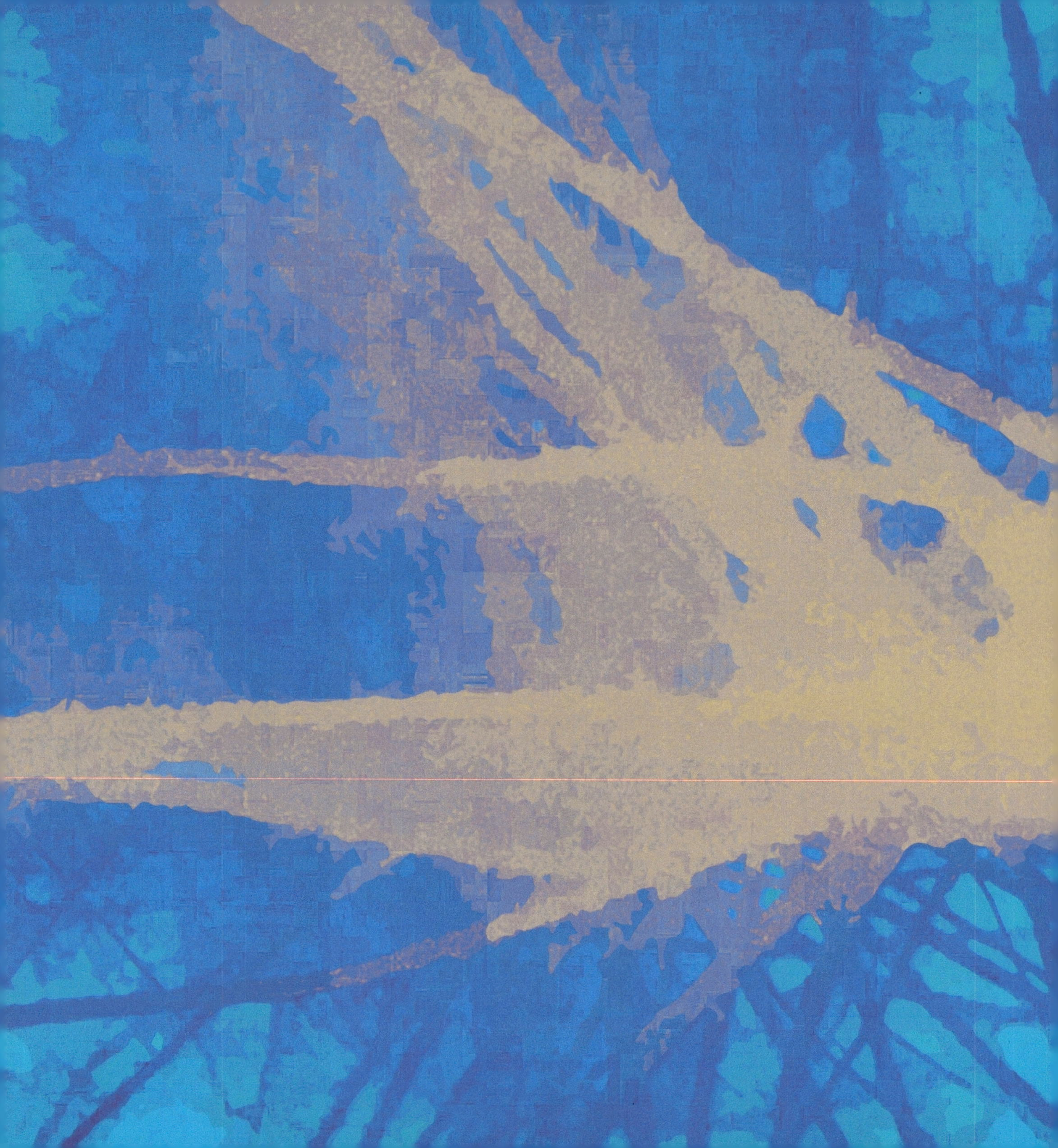

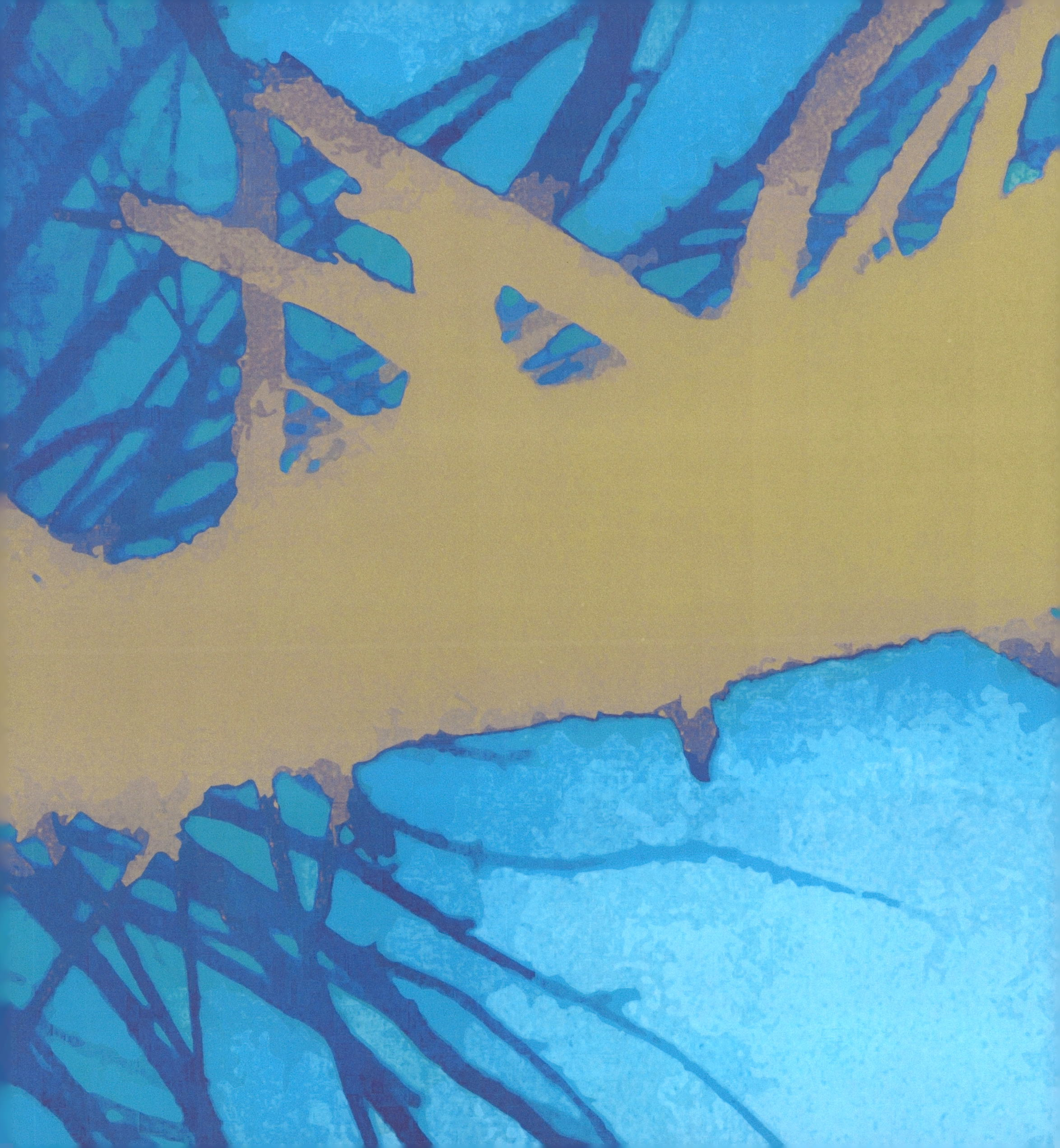

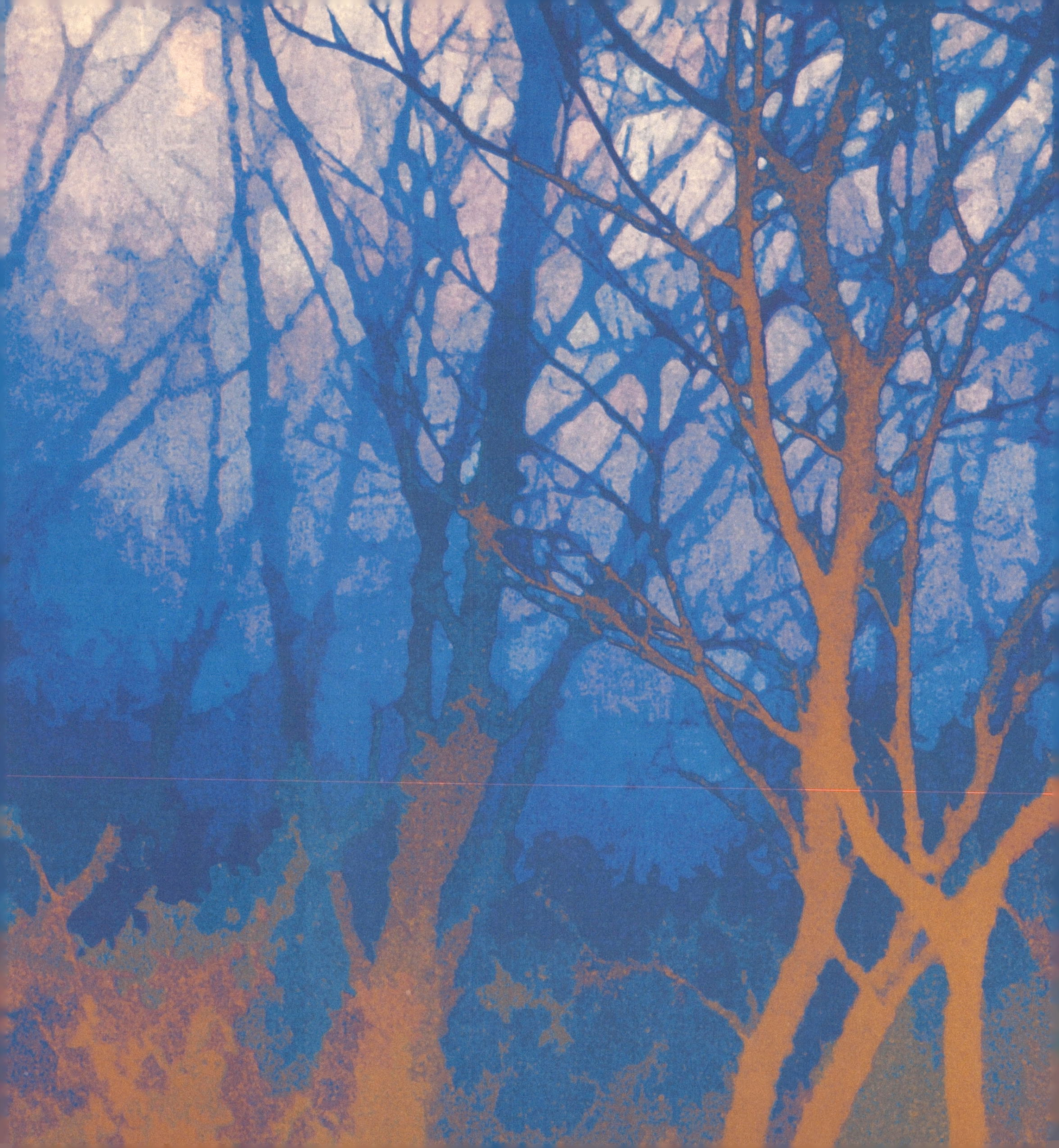

Here, nestled—

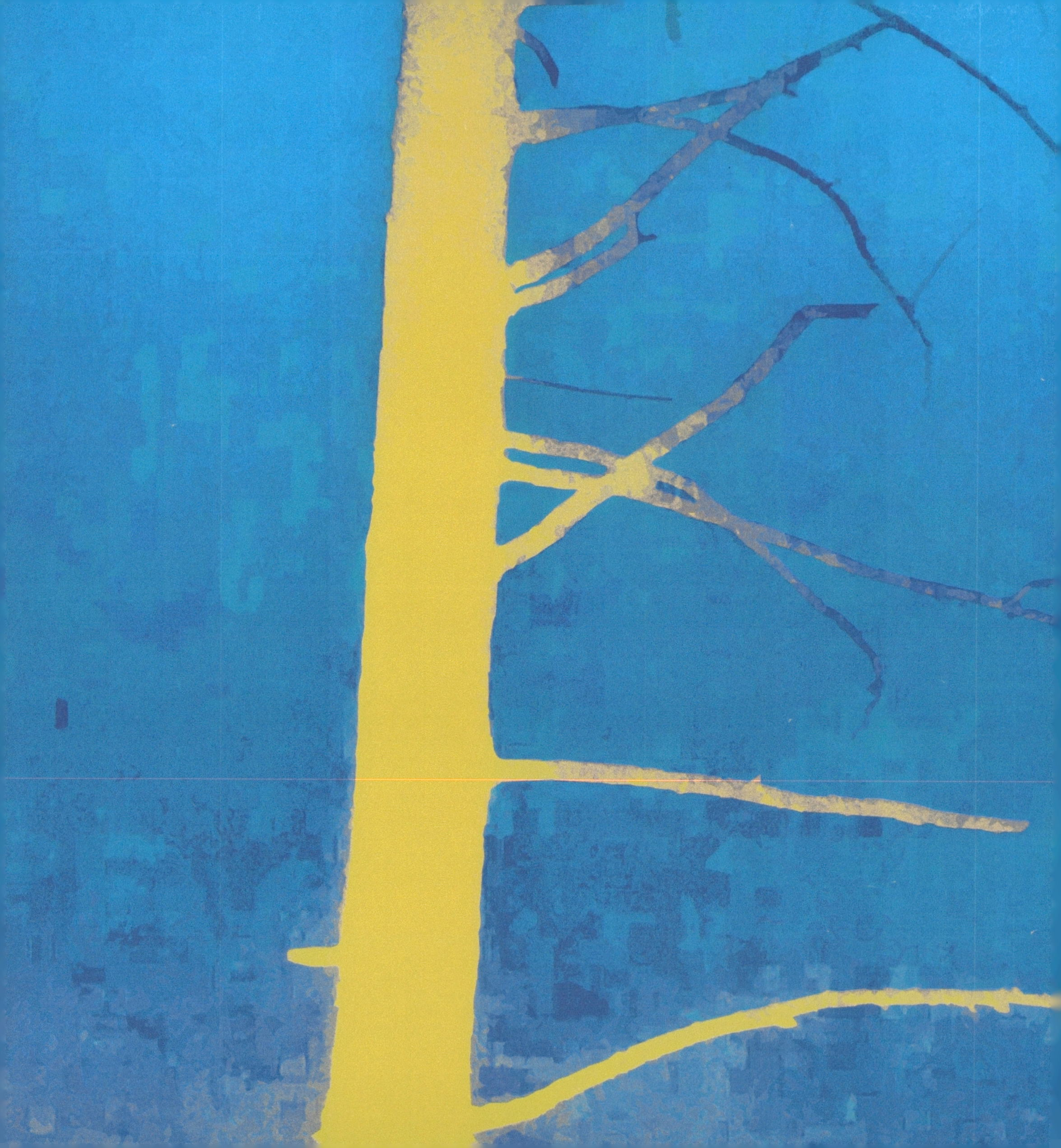

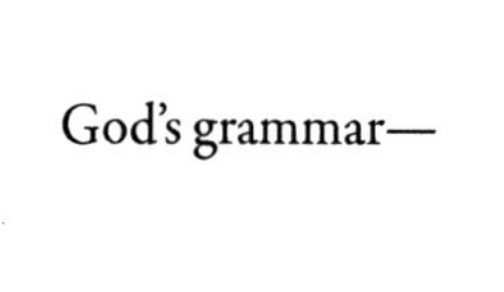

God’s grammar—

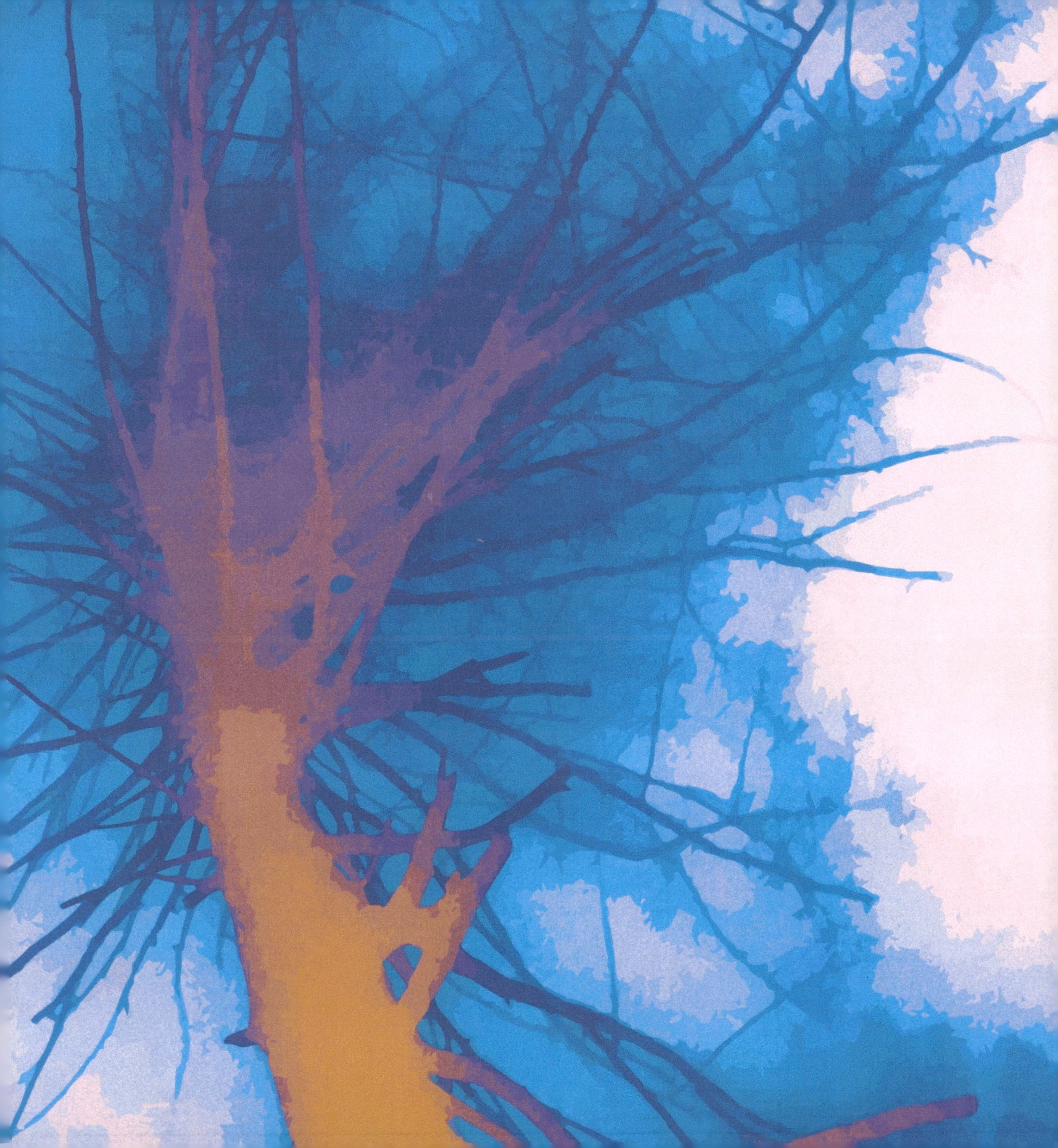

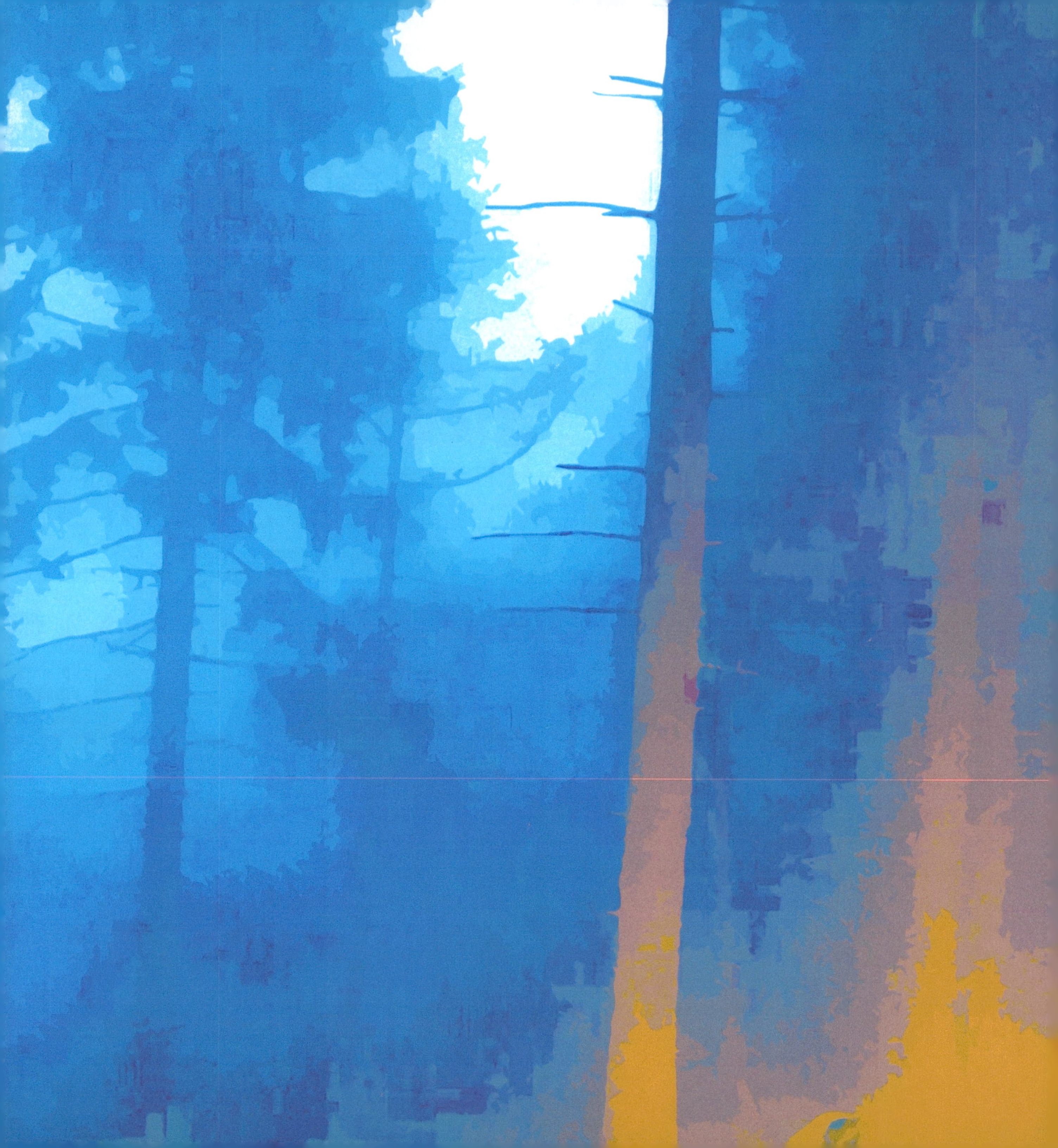

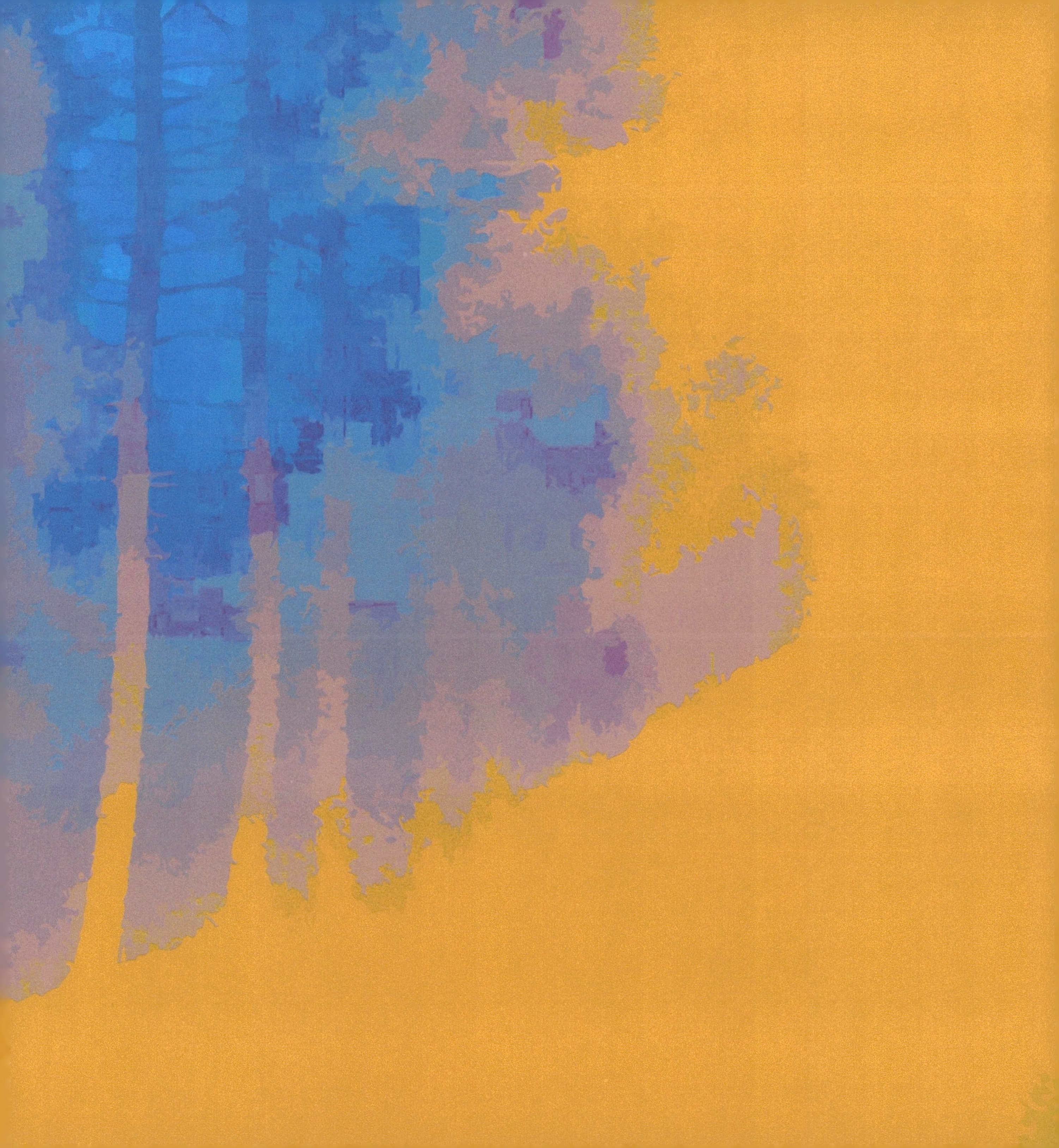

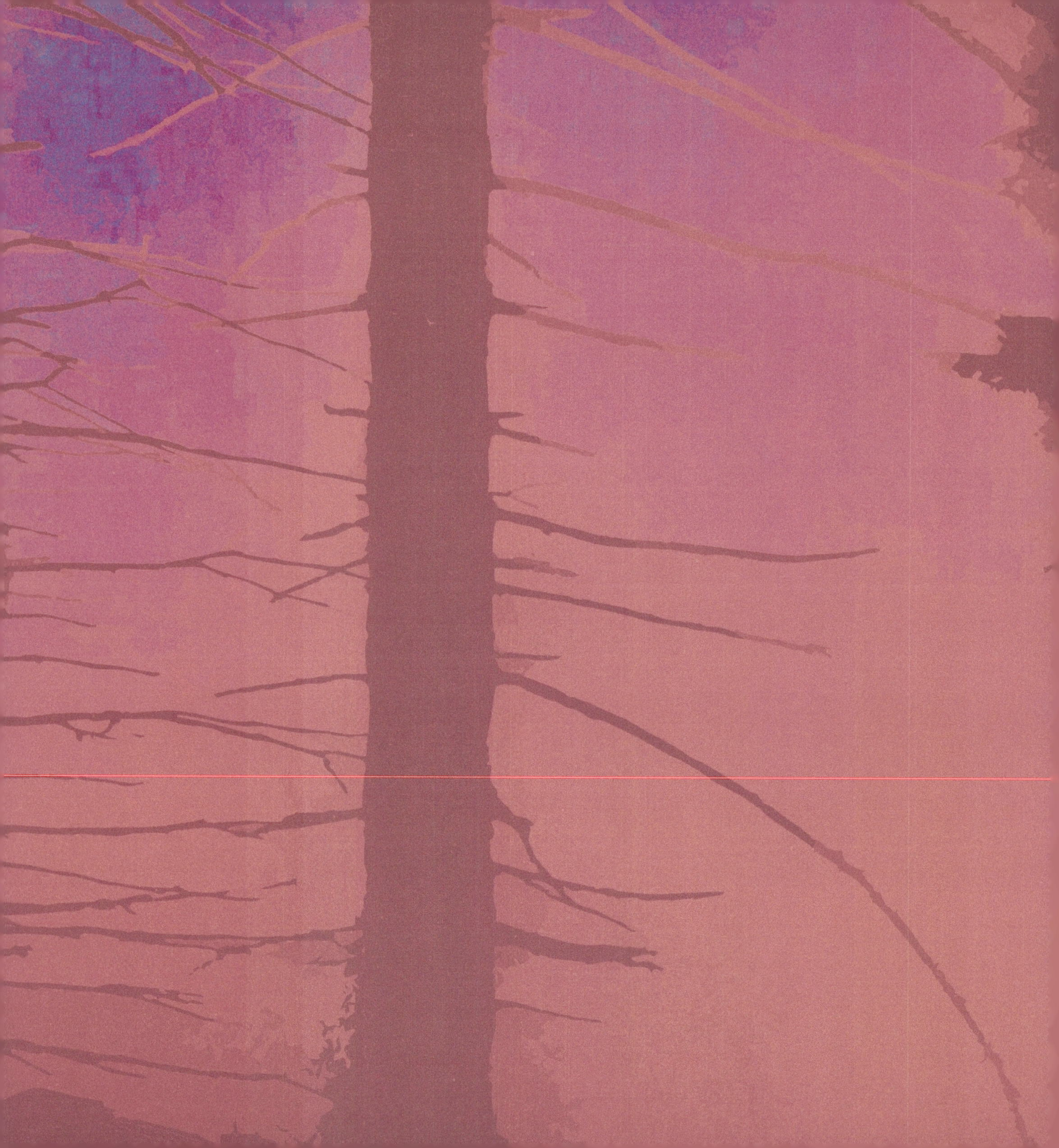

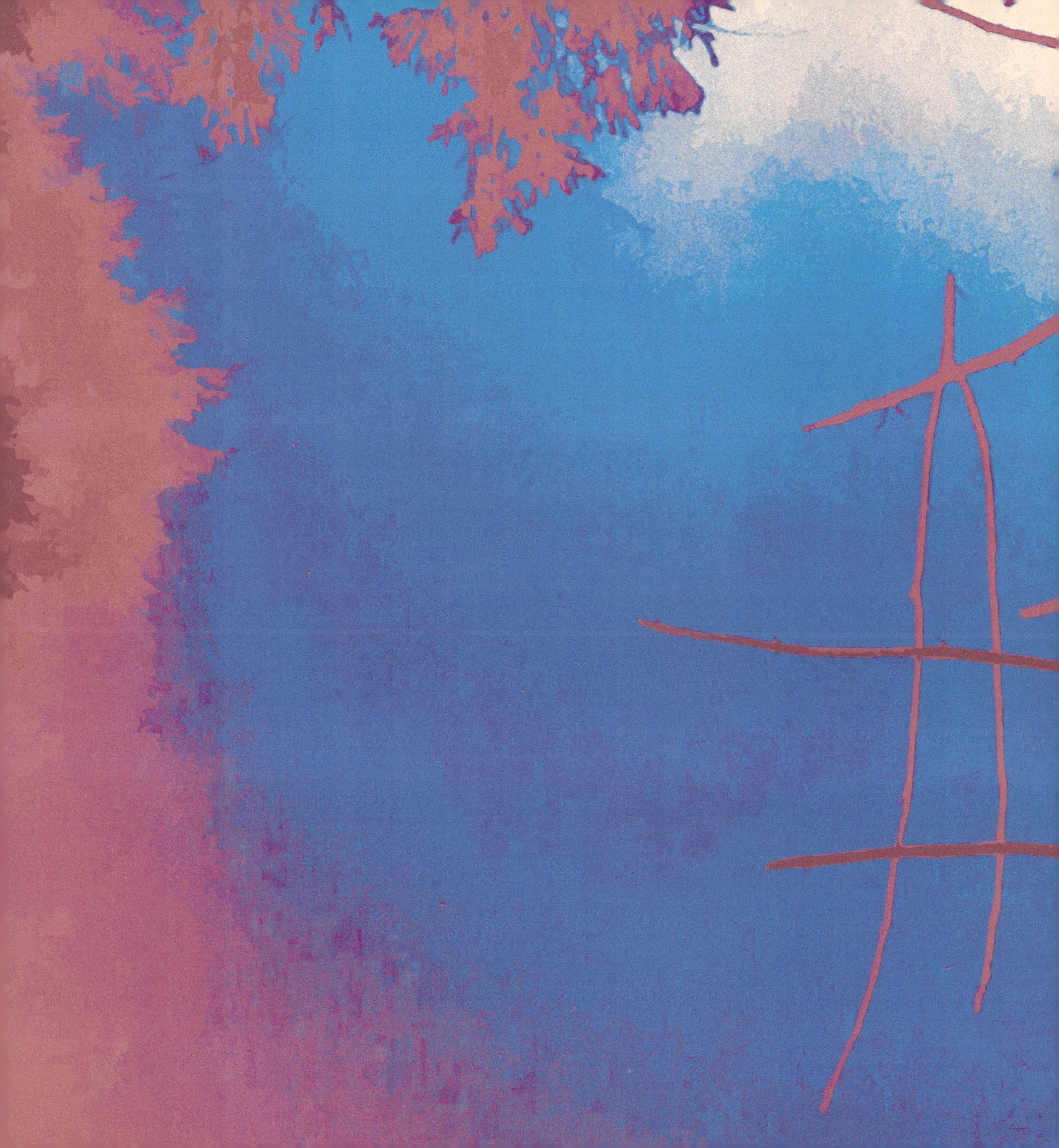

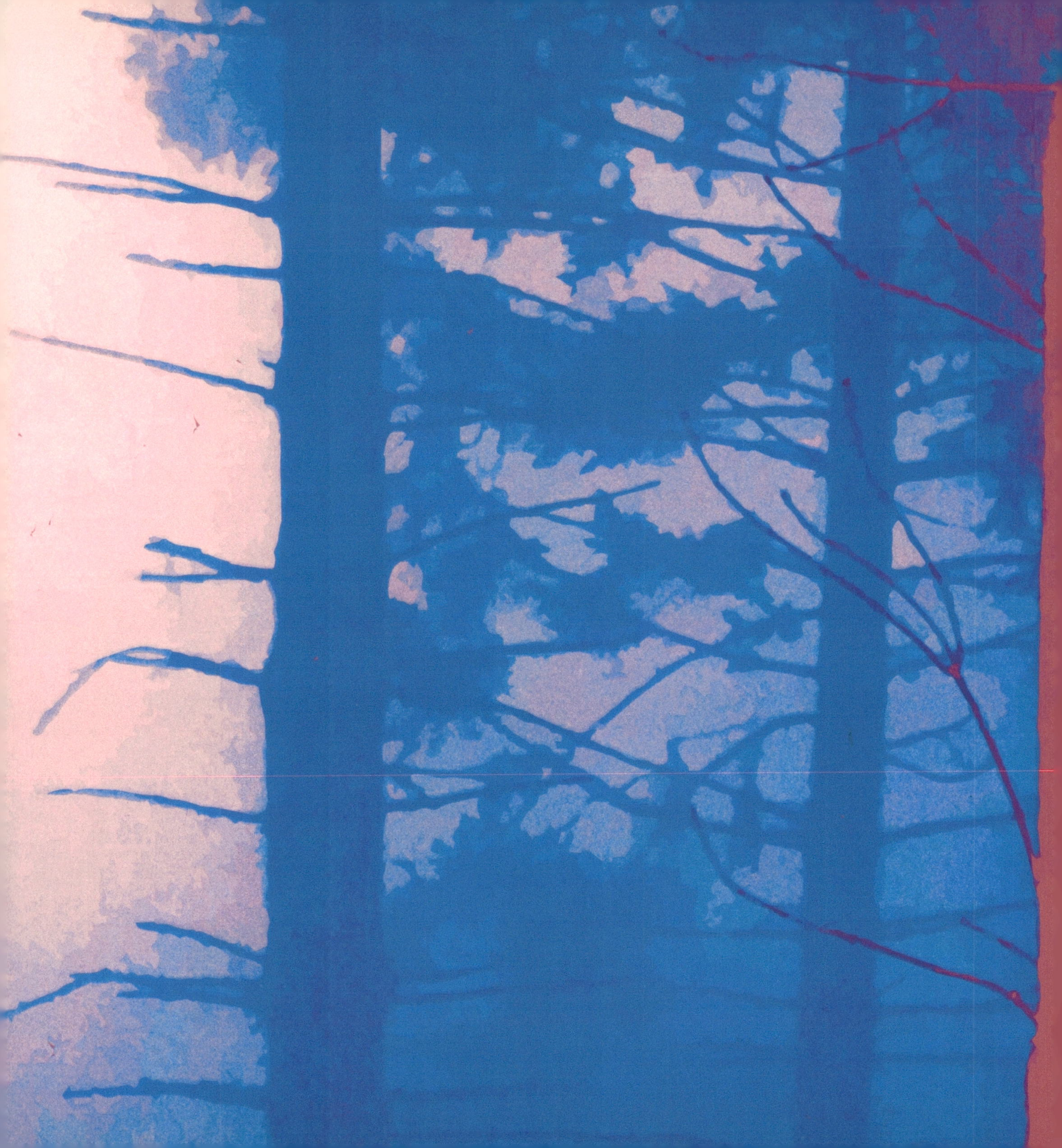

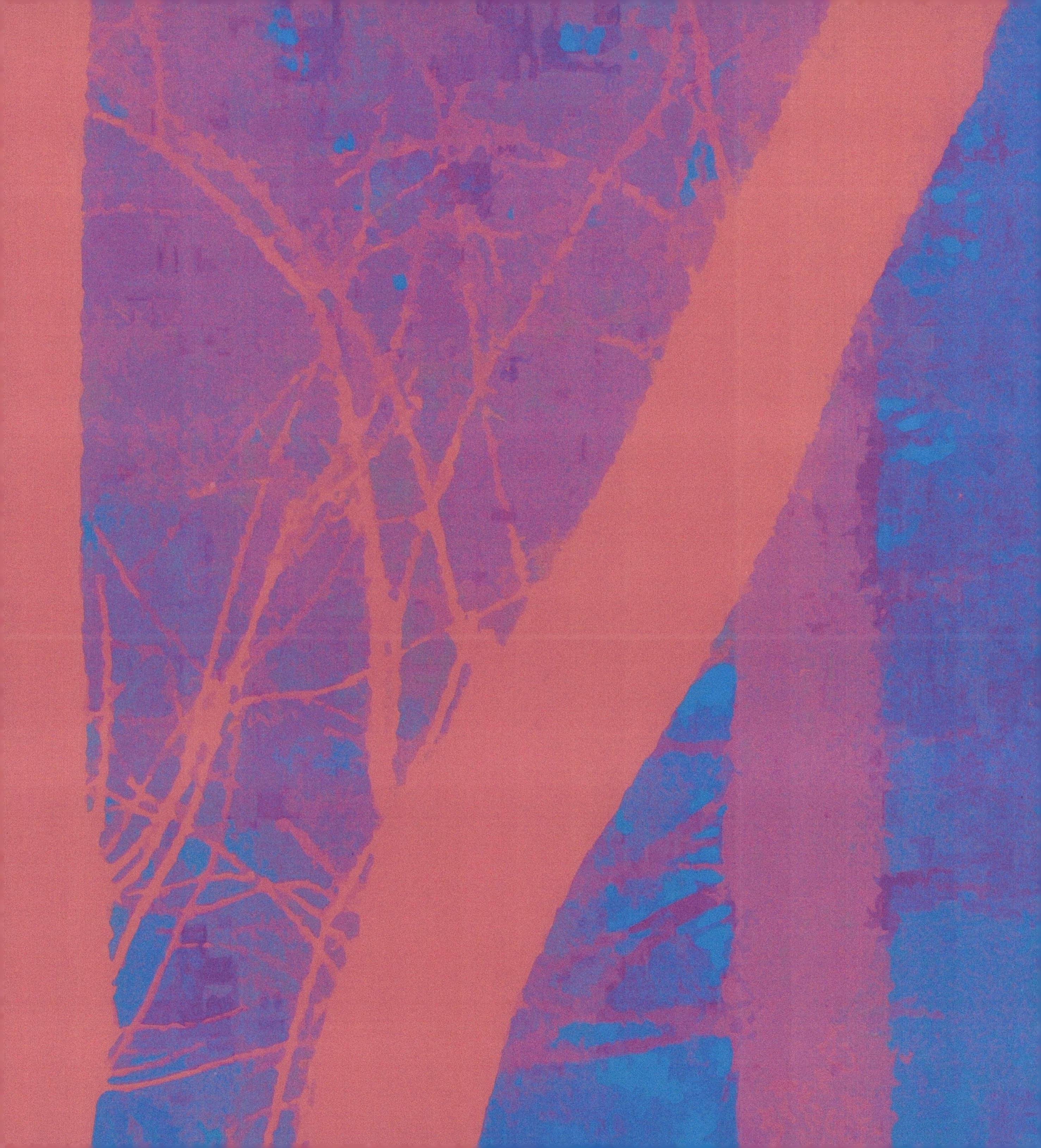

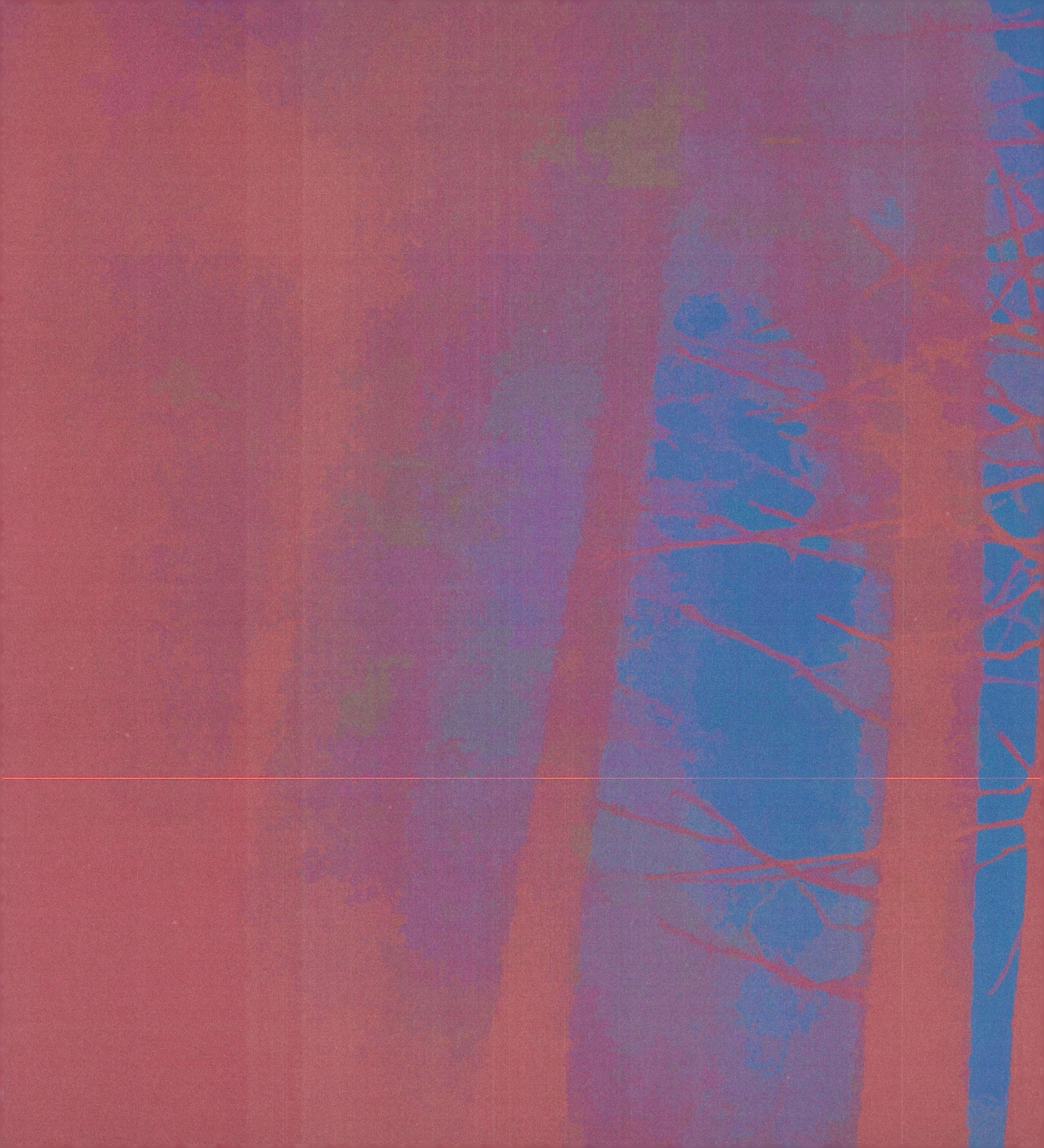

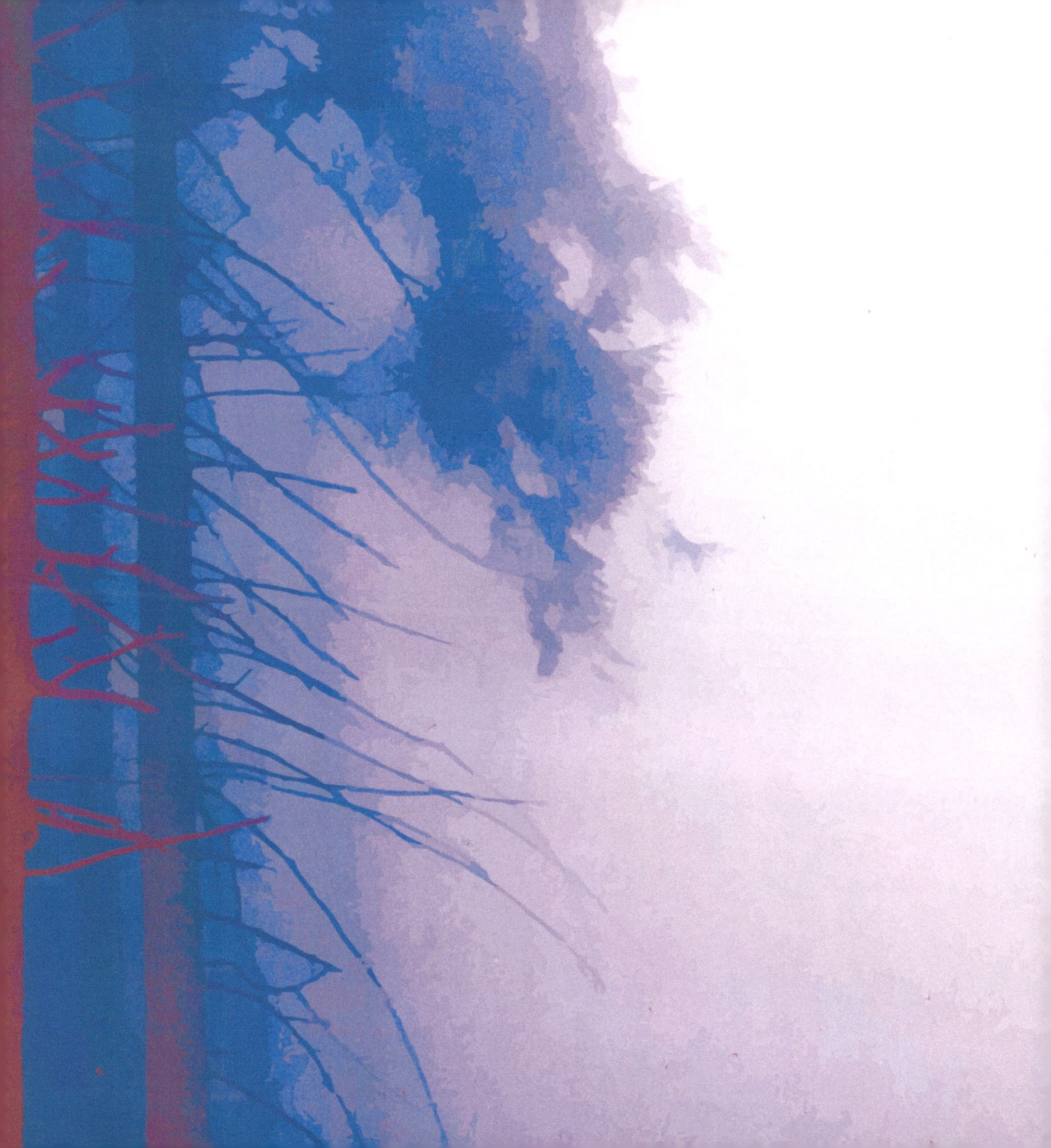

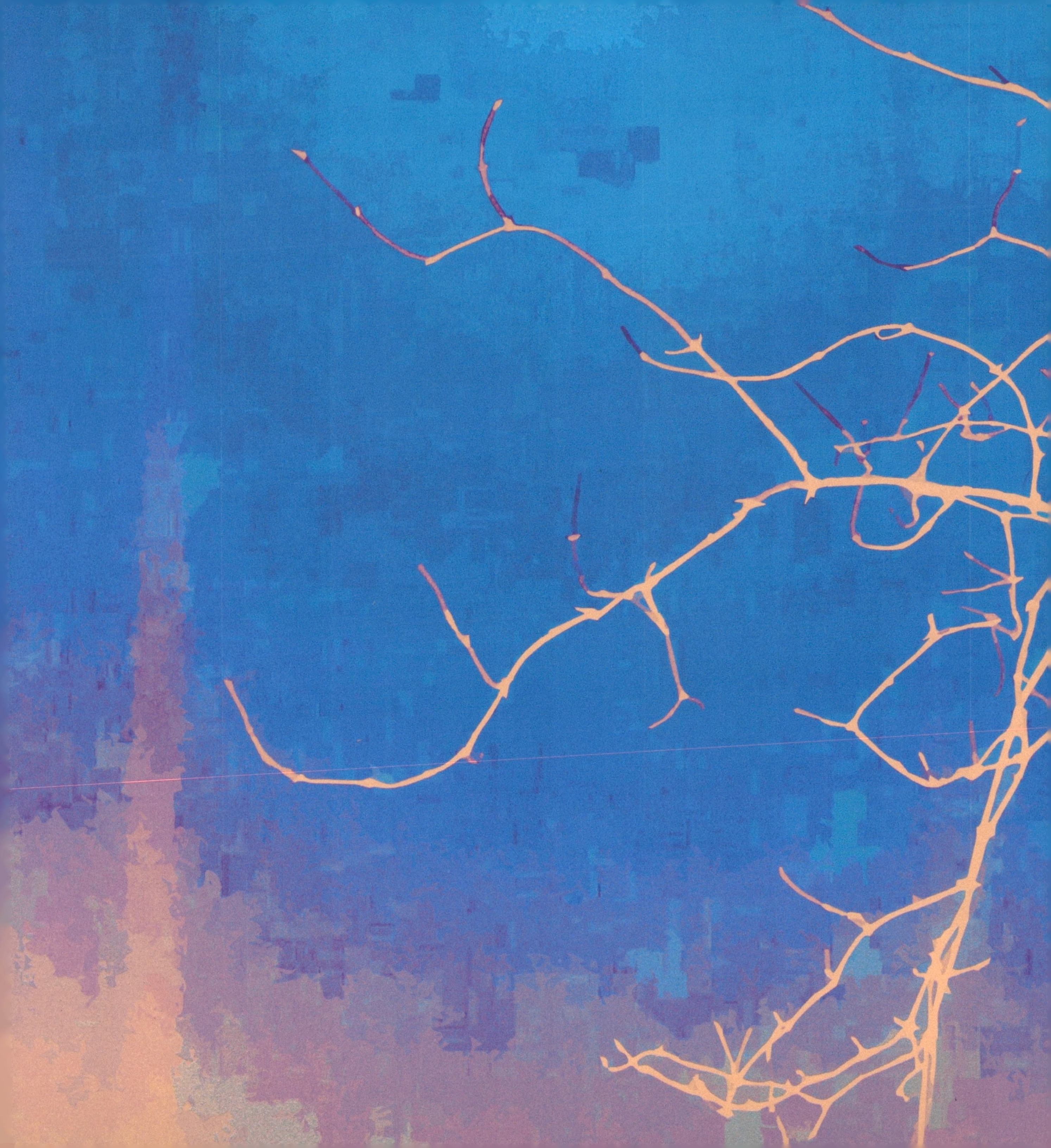

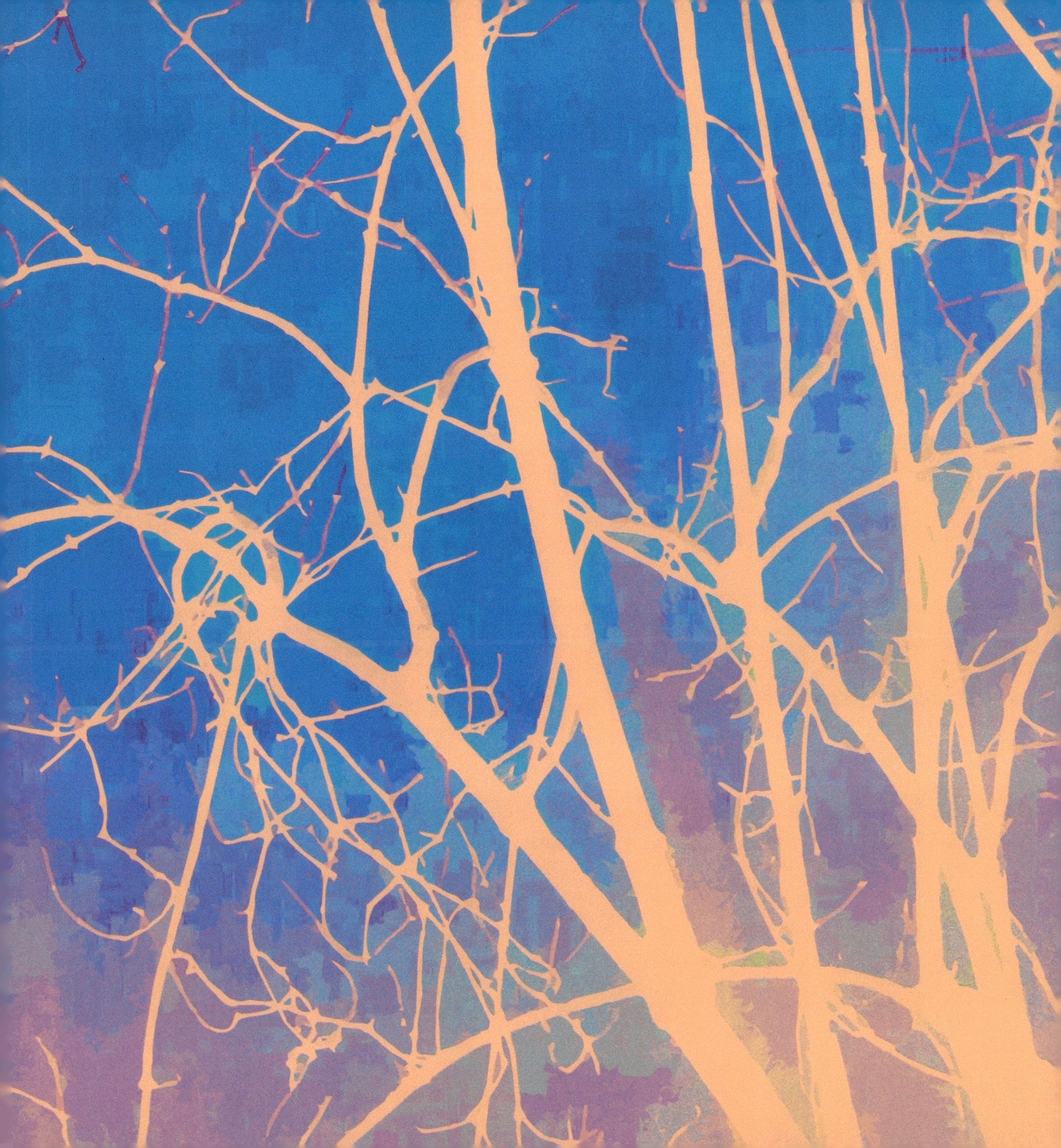

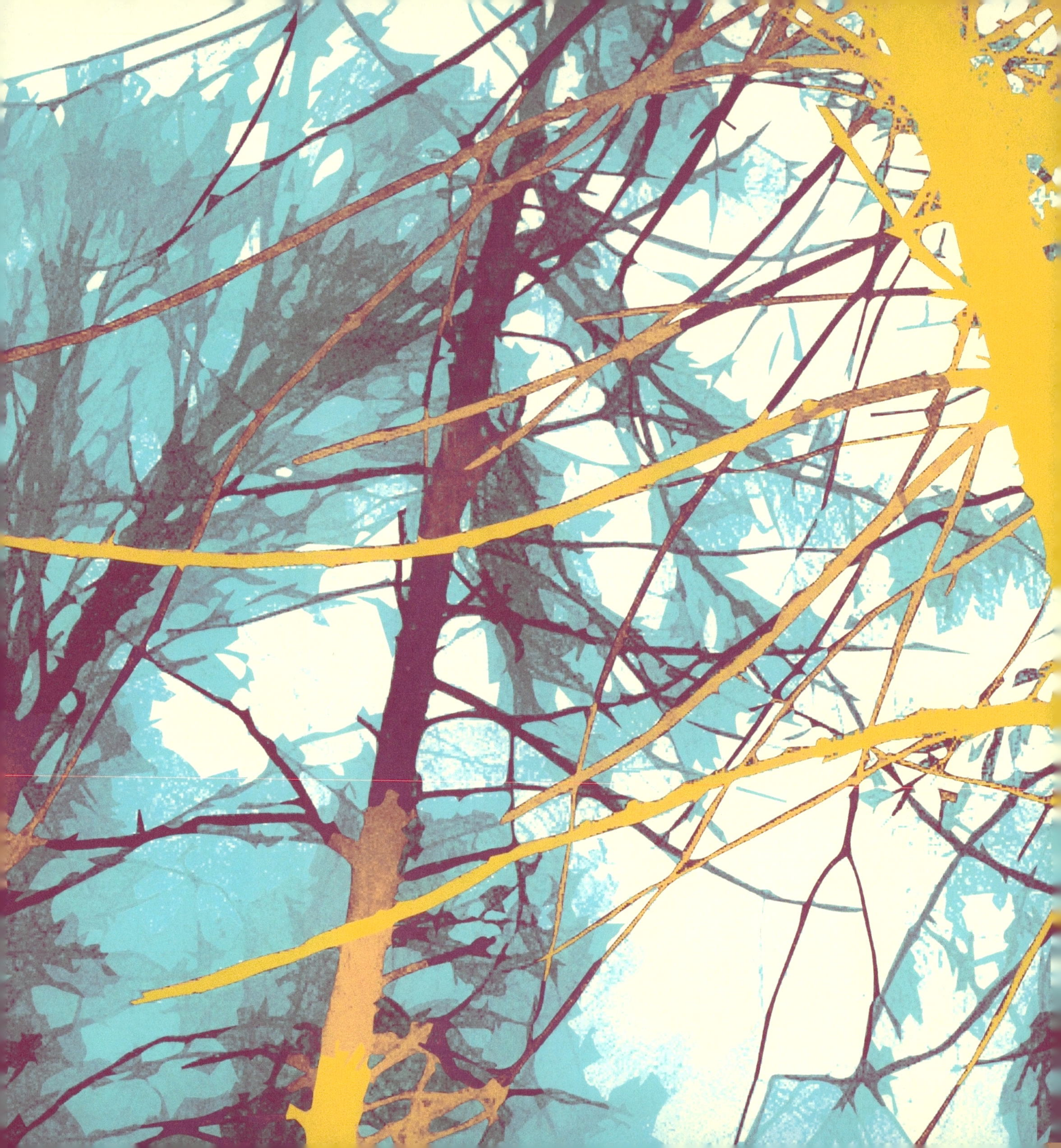

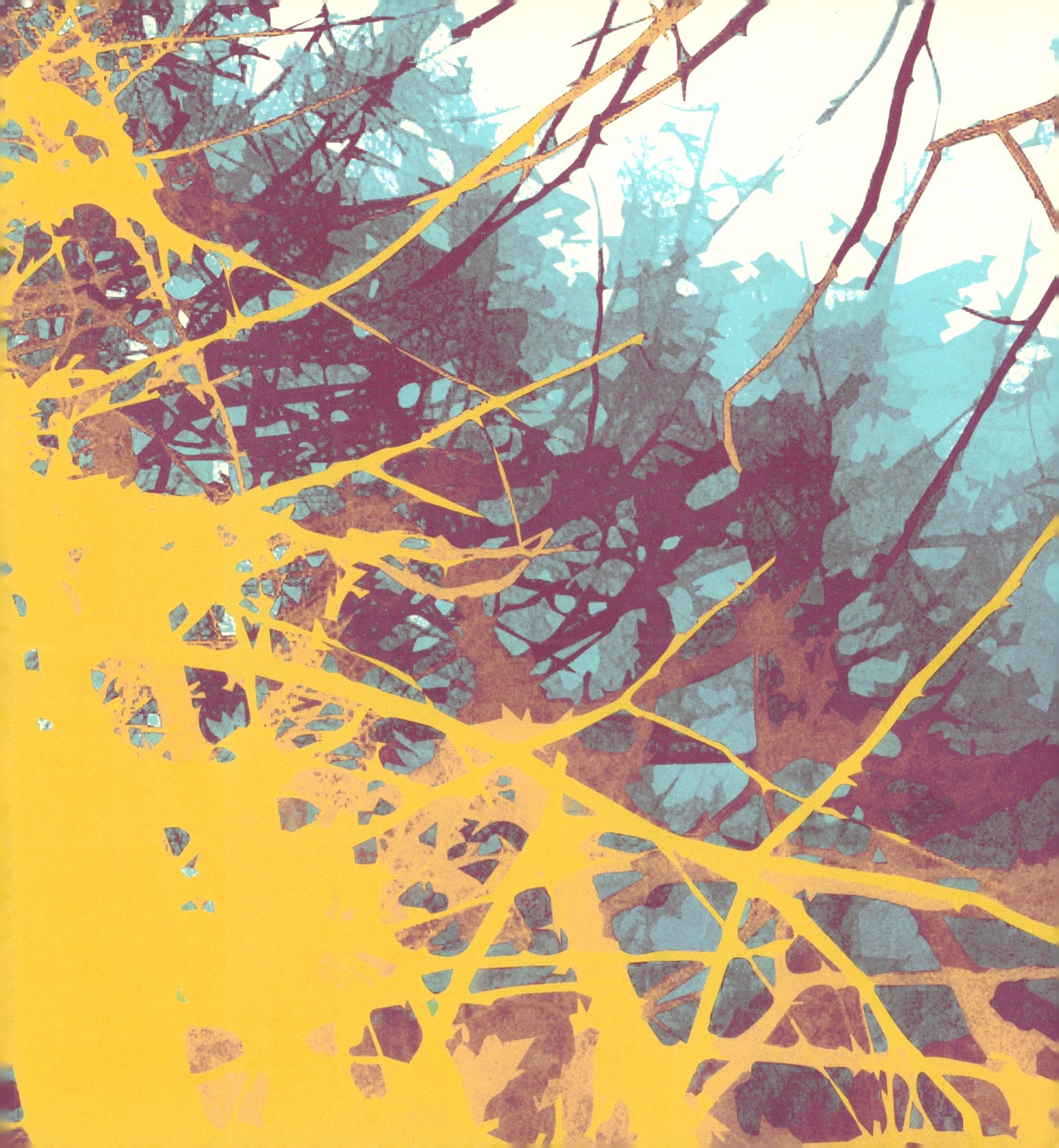

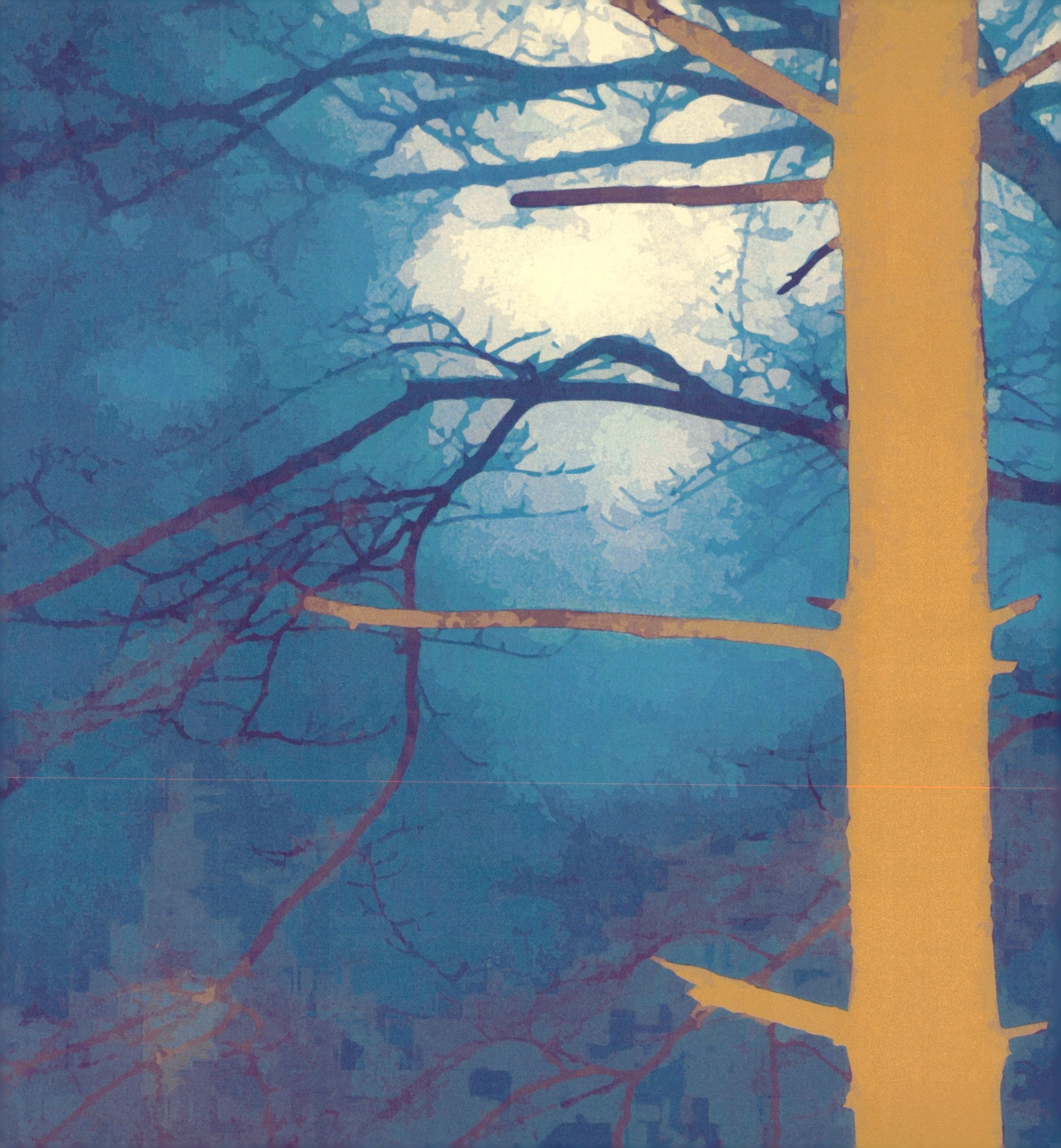

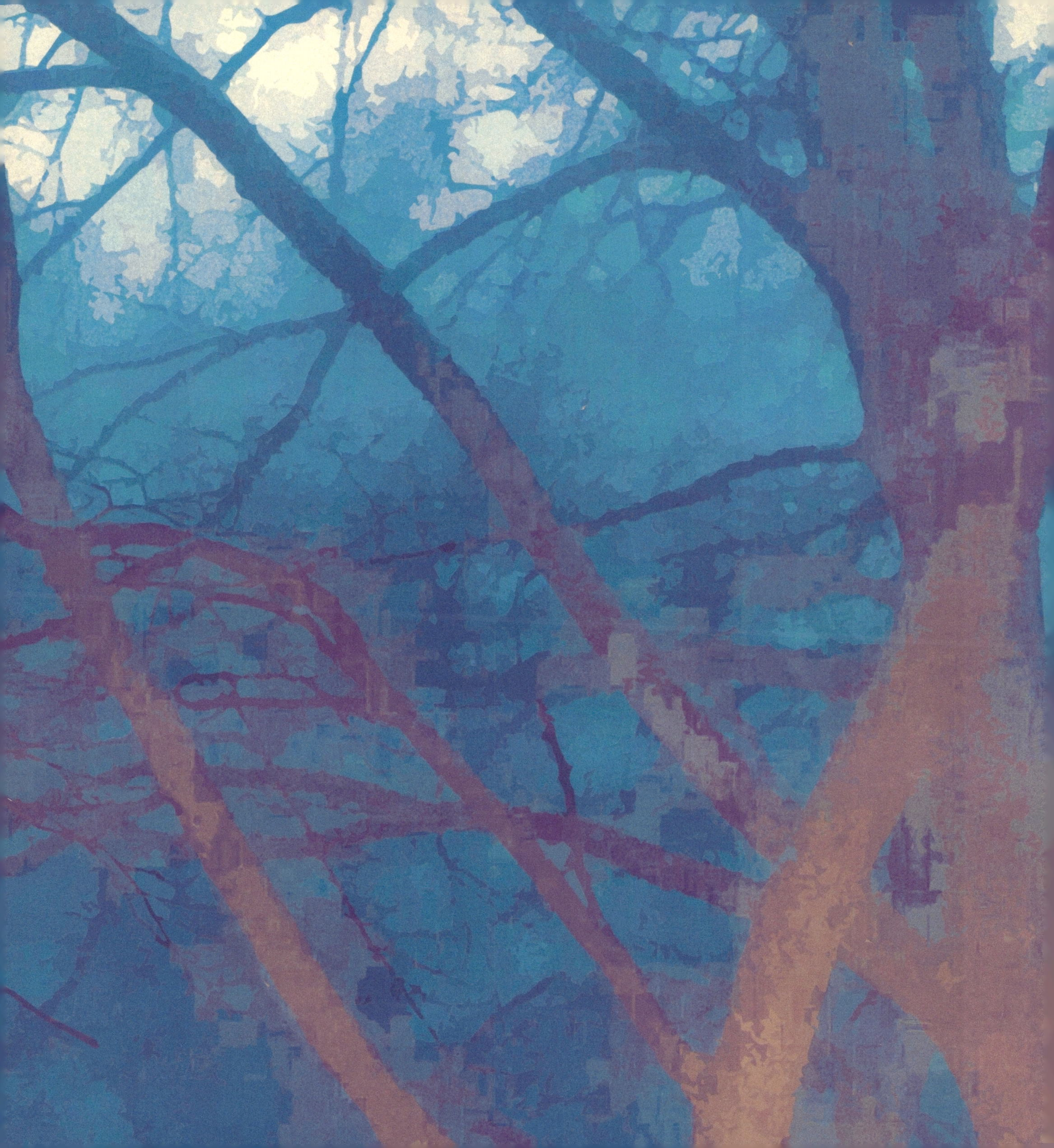

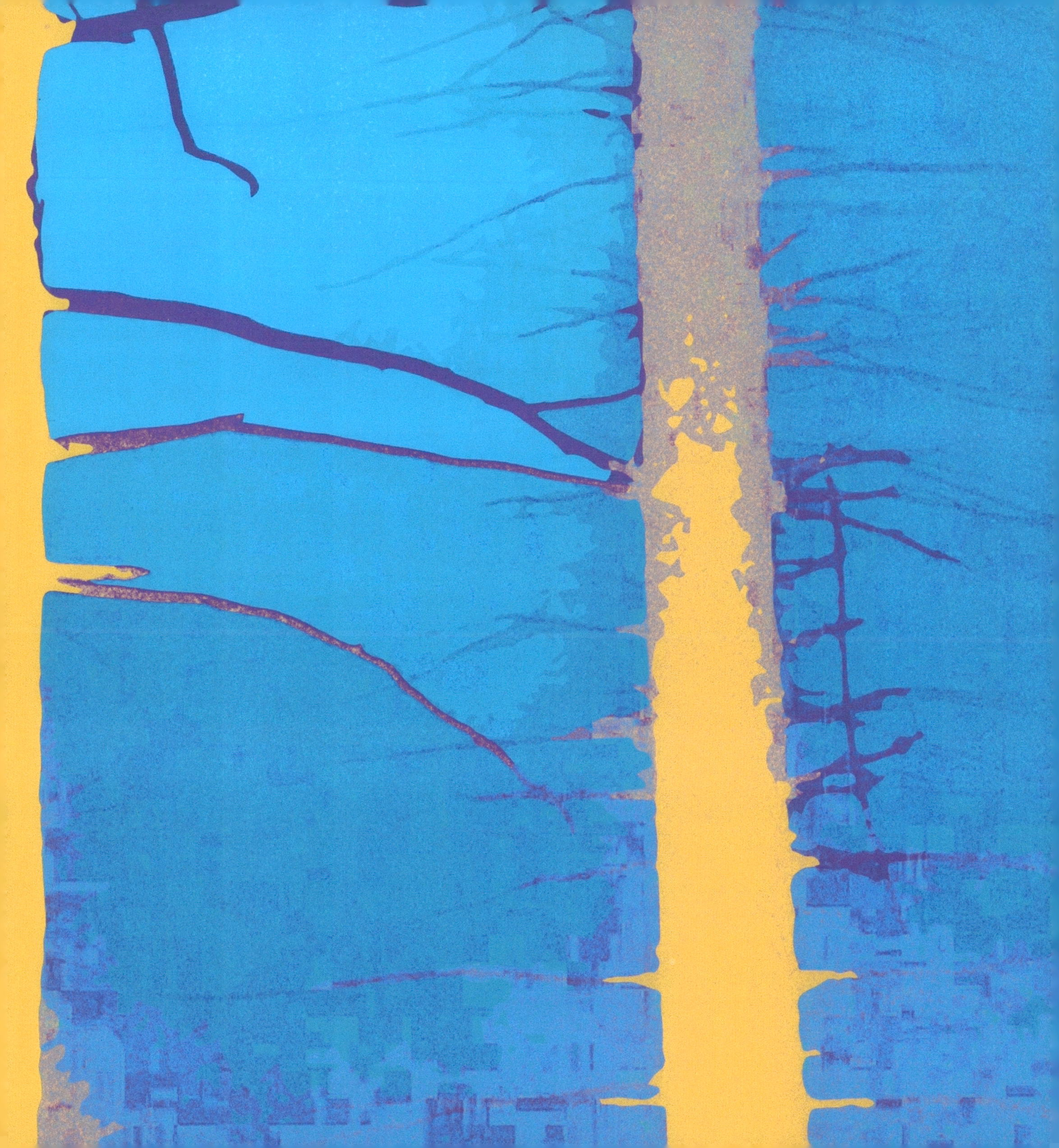

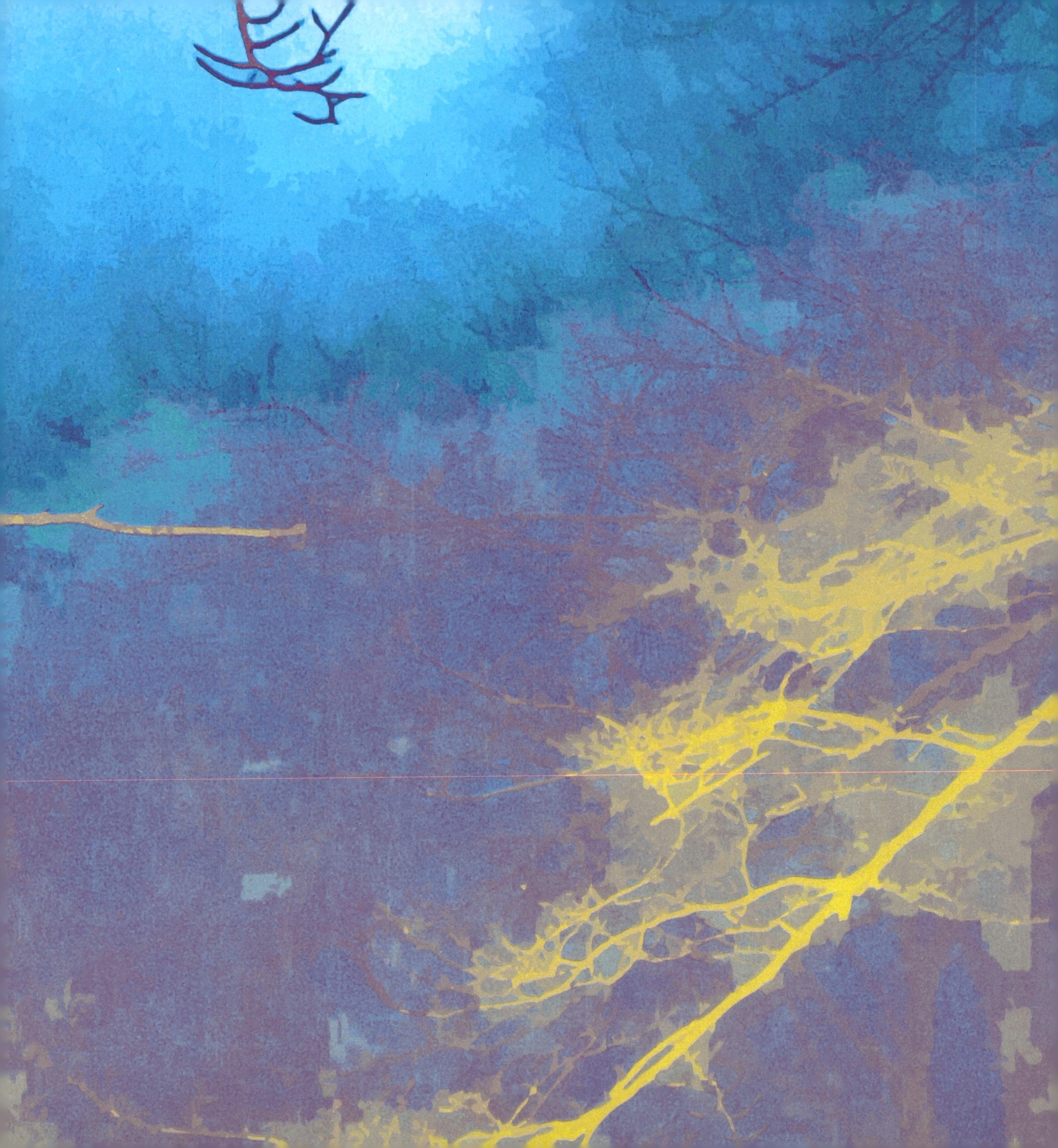

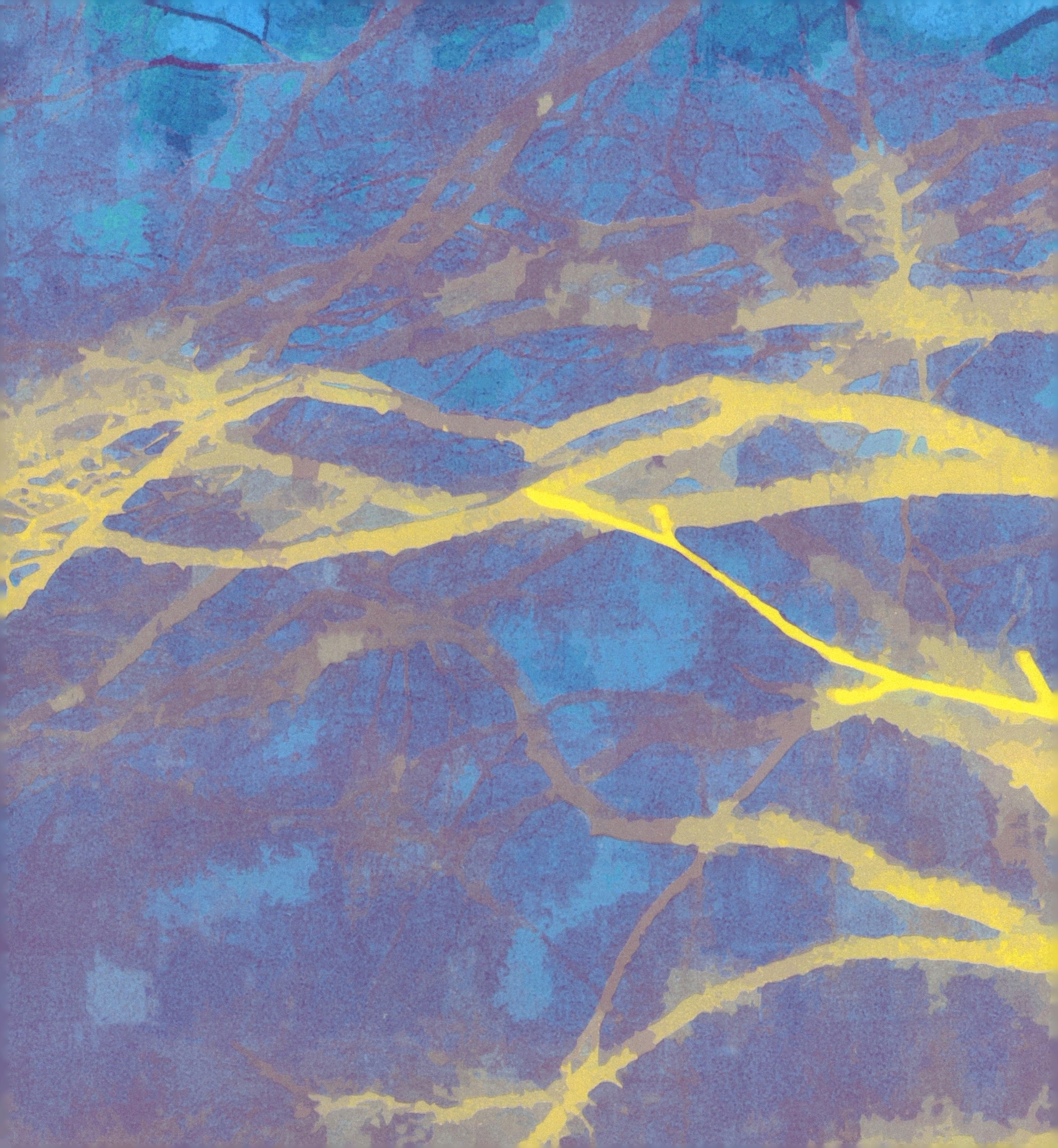

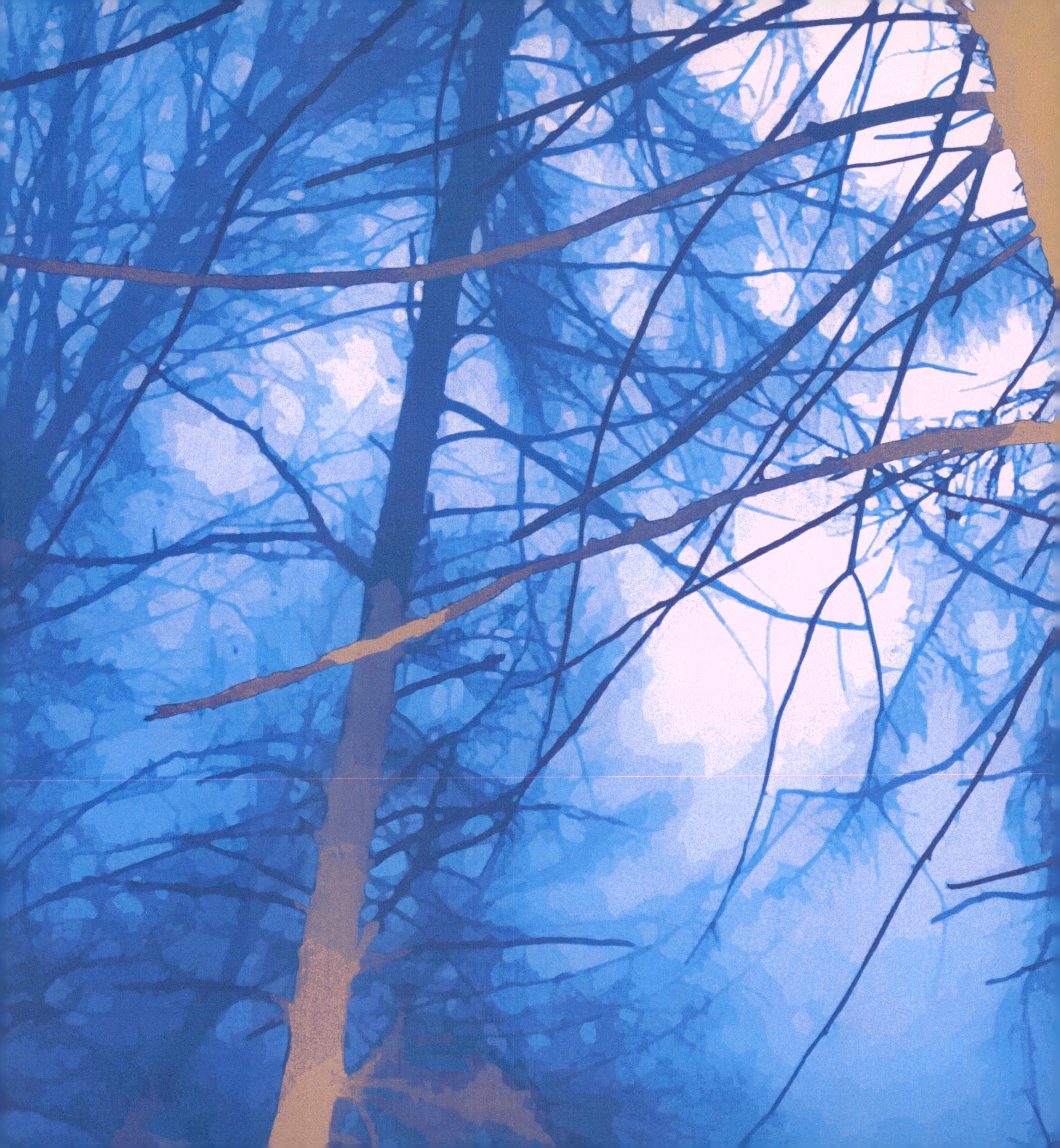

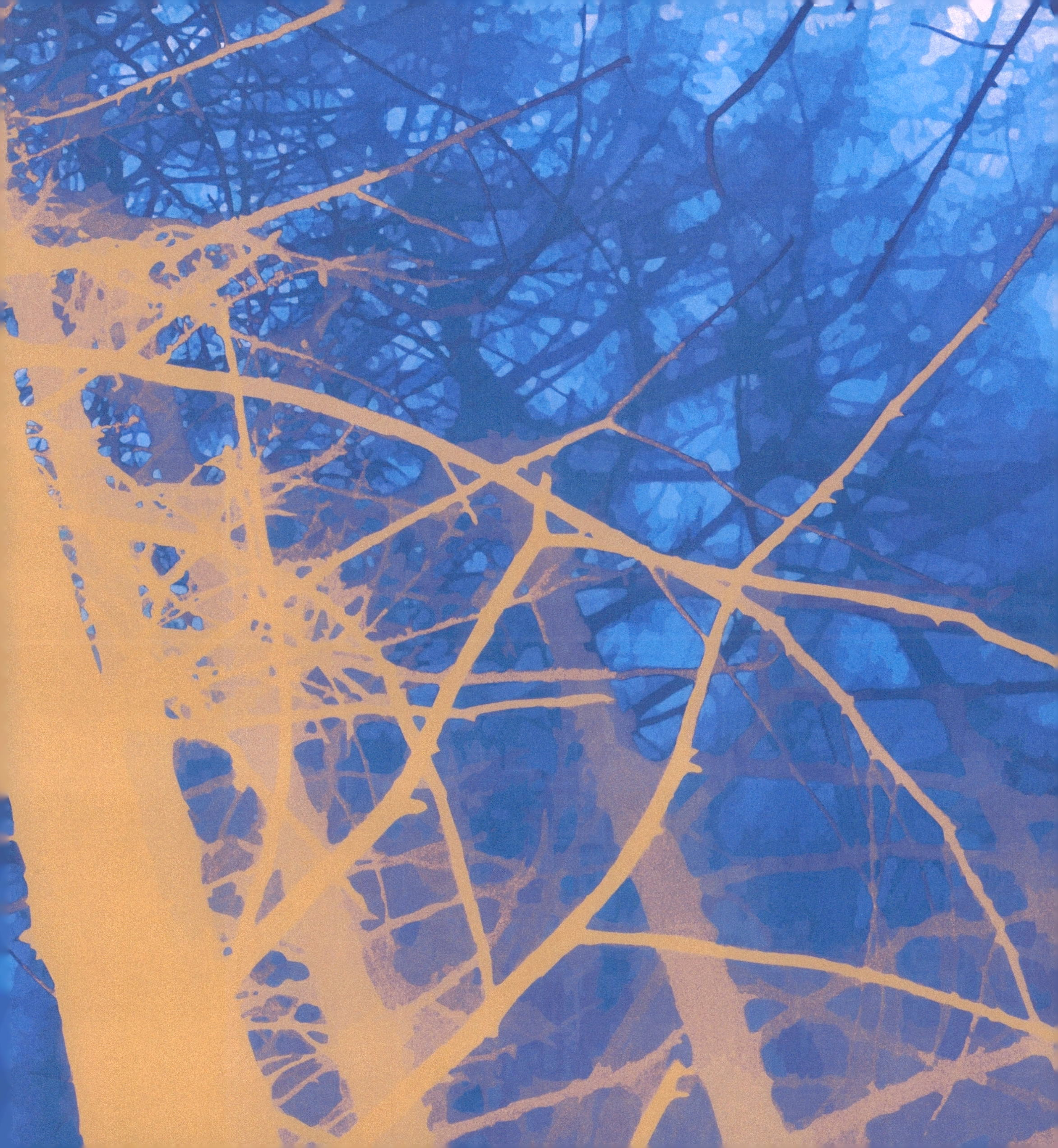

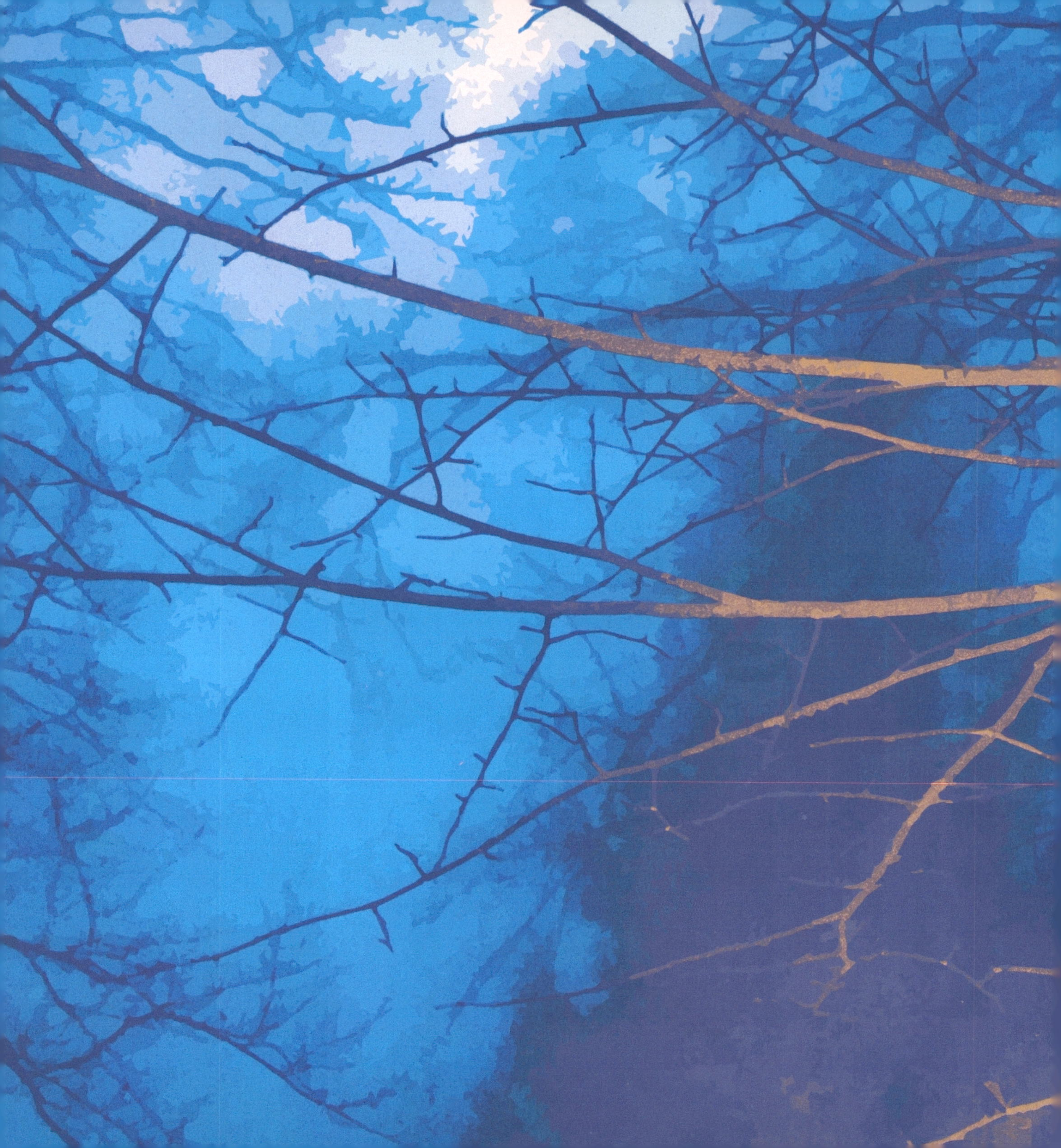

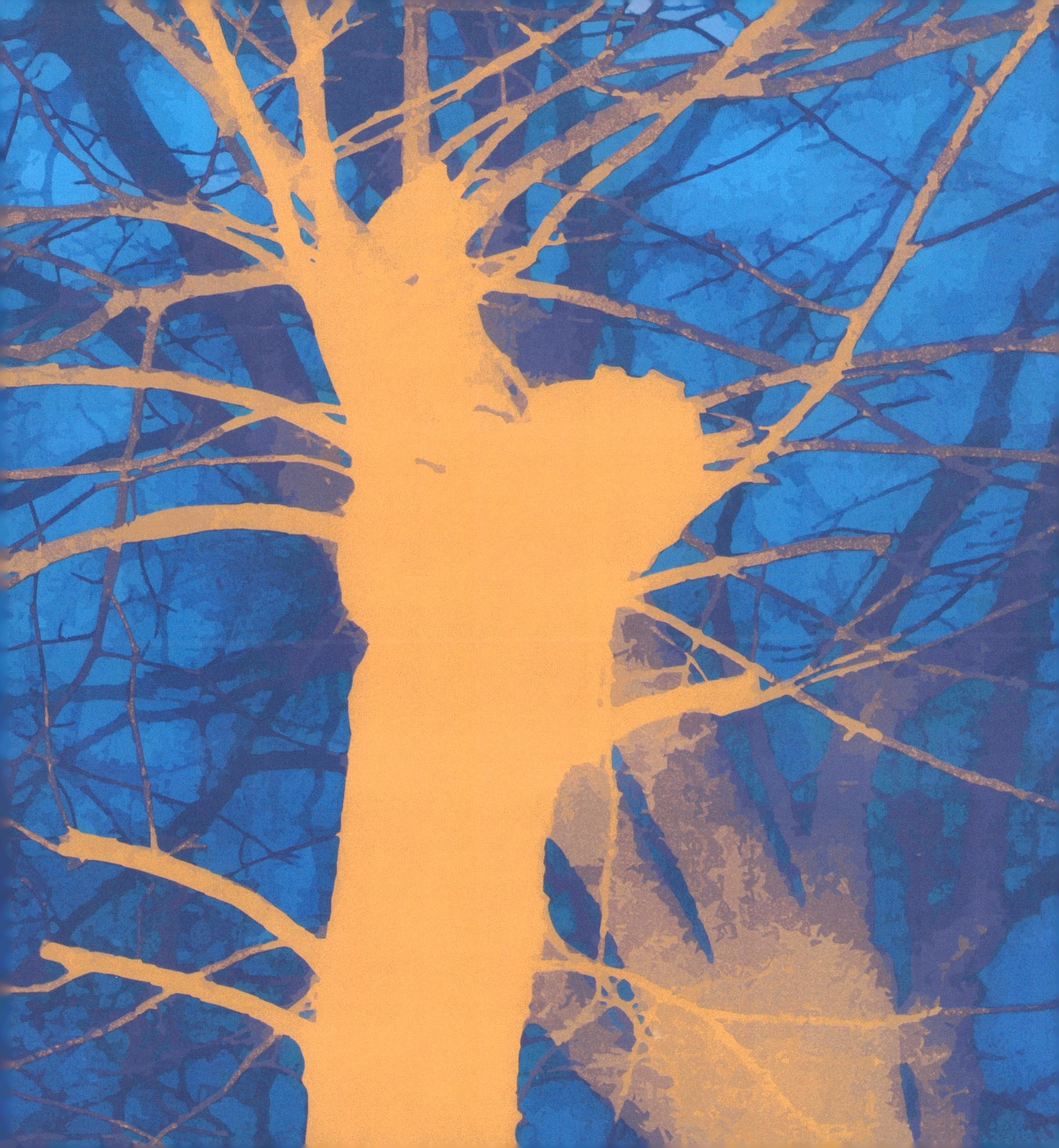

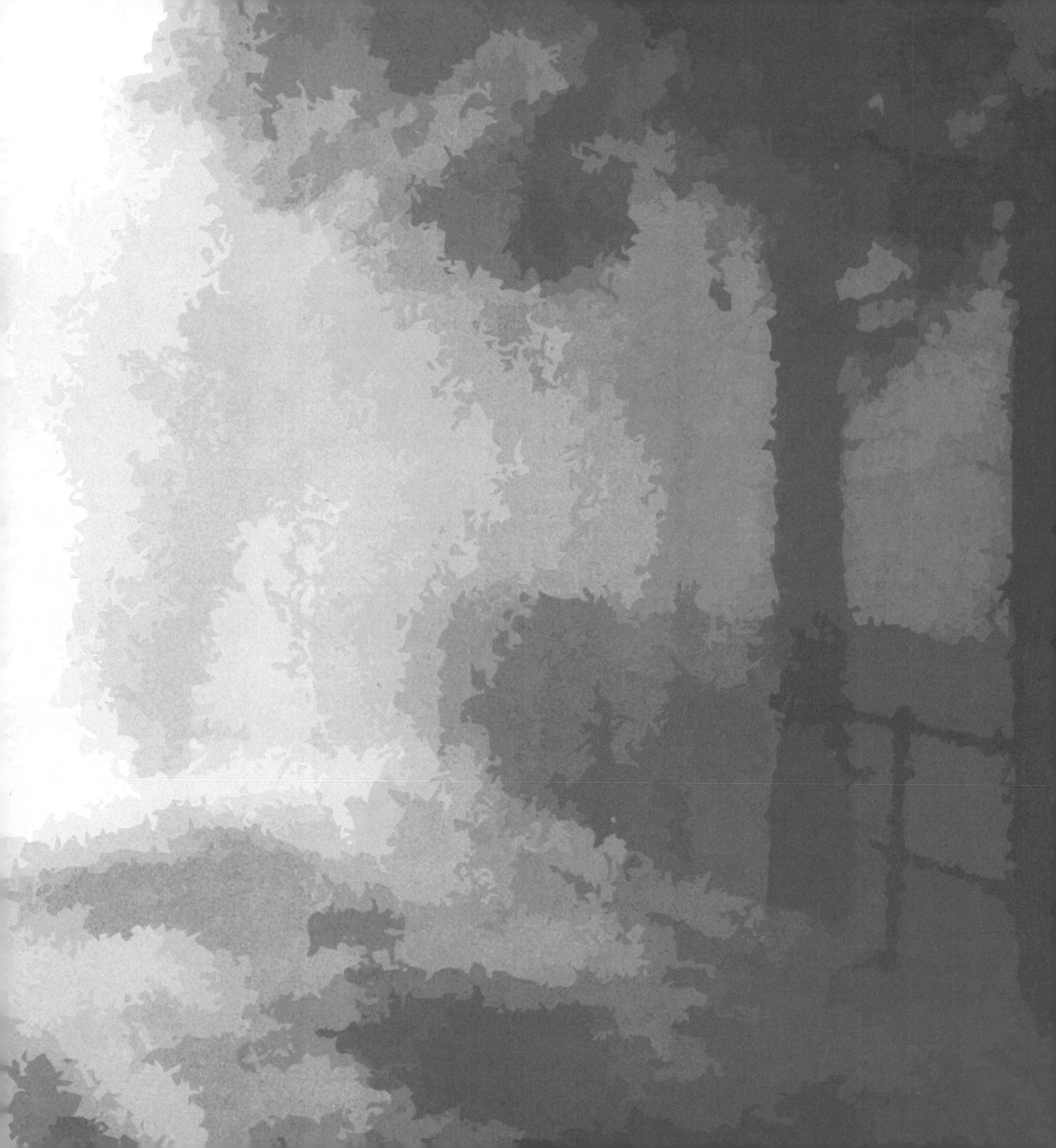

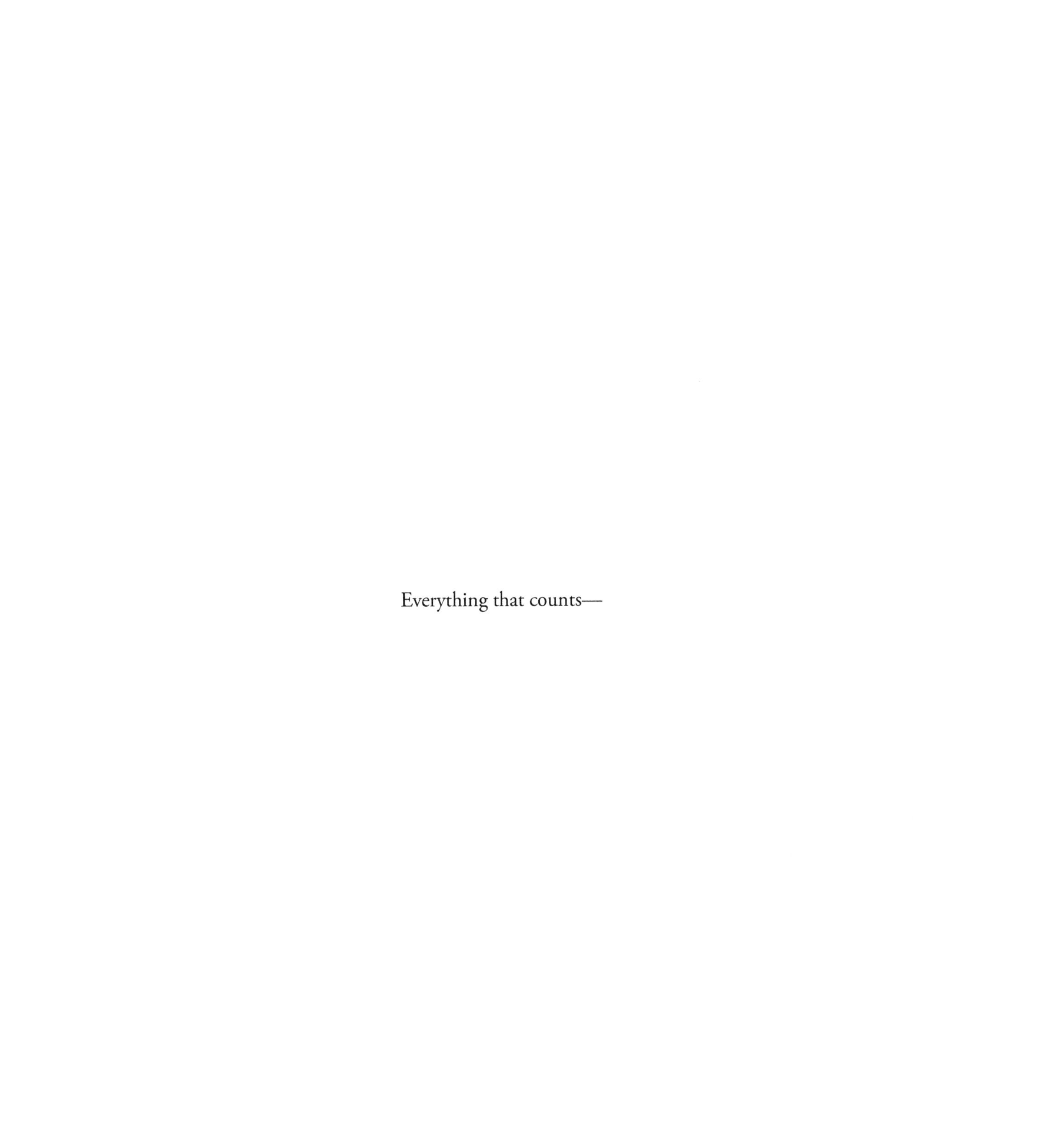

Everything that counts—

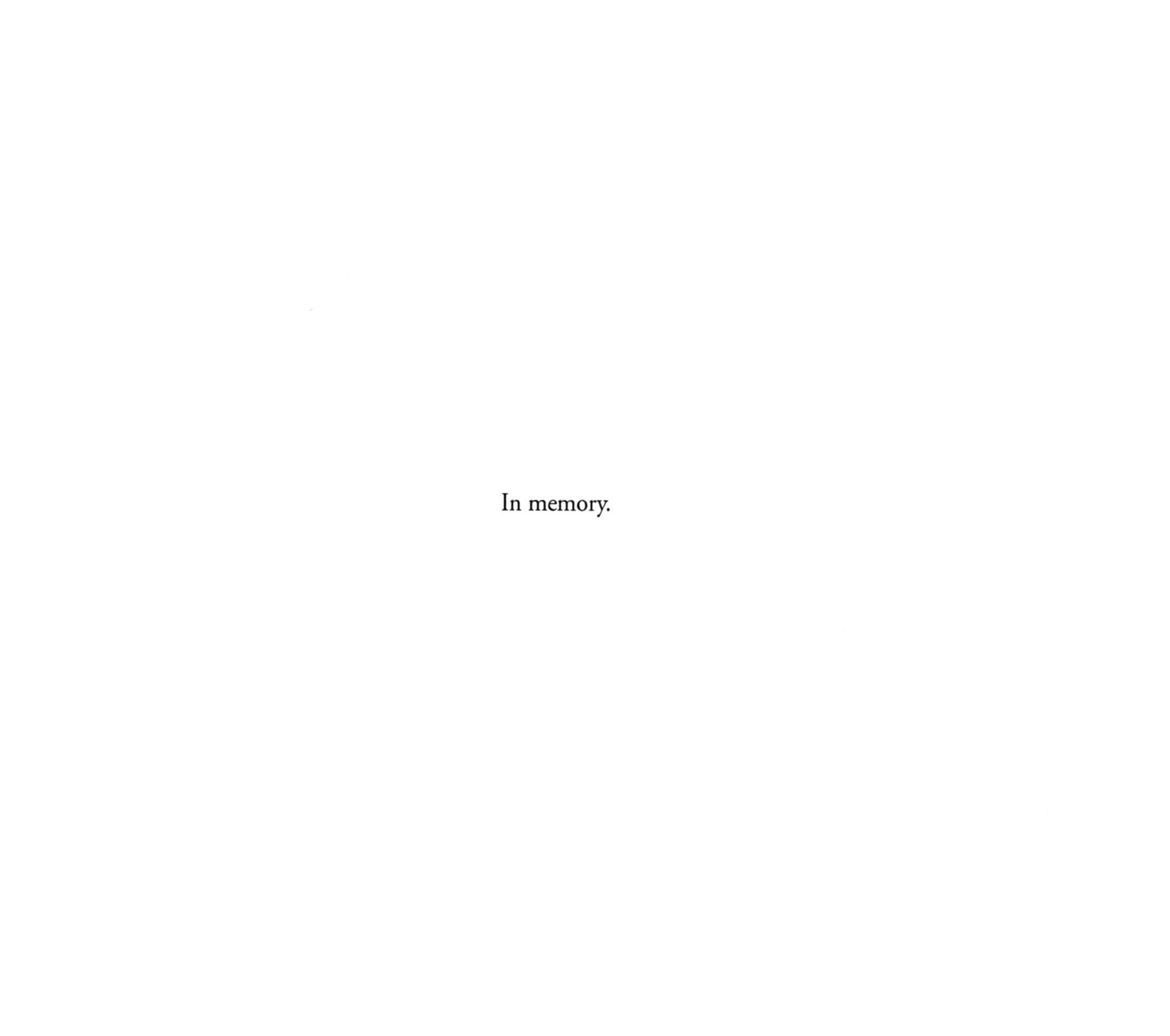

In memory.

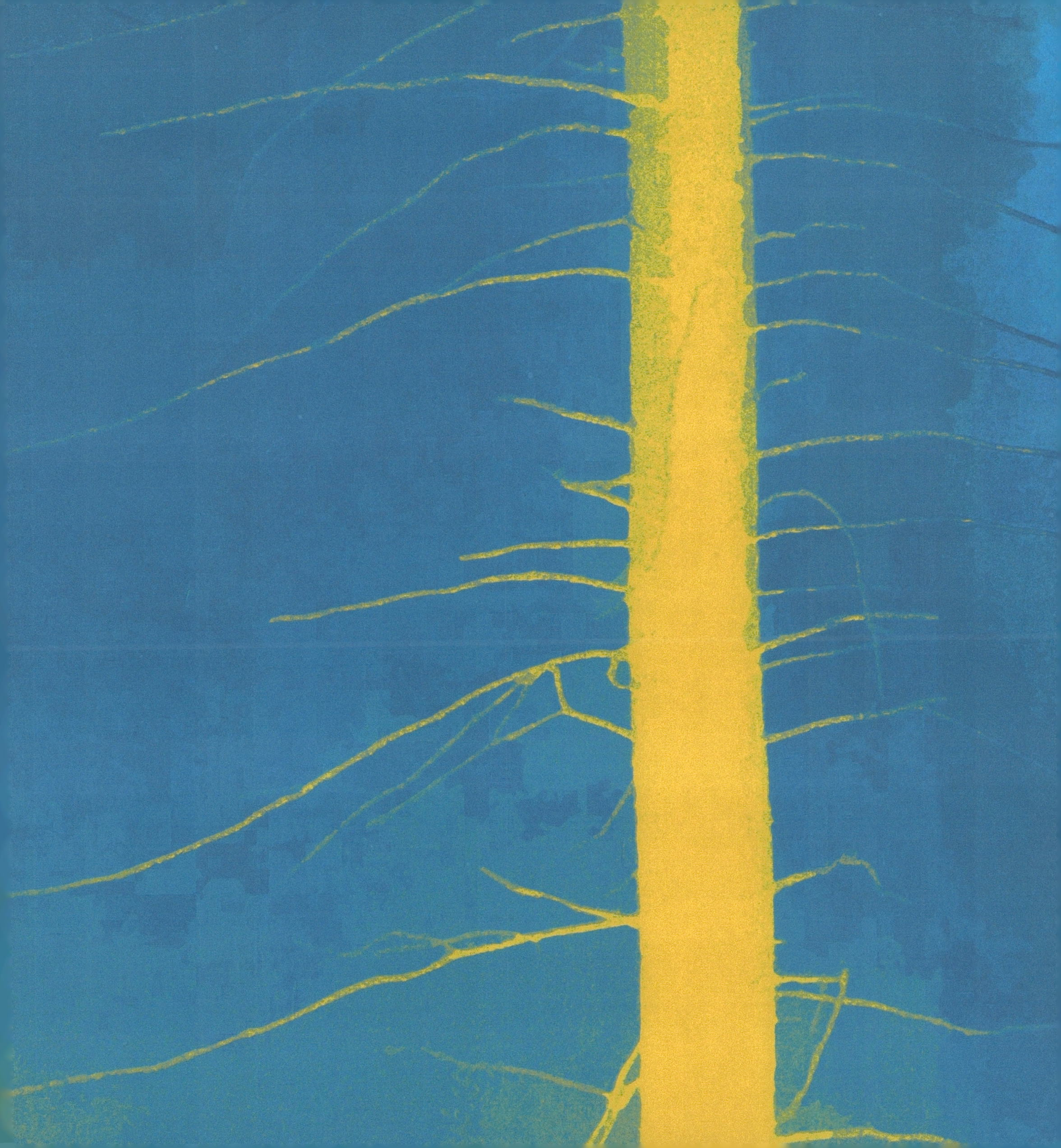

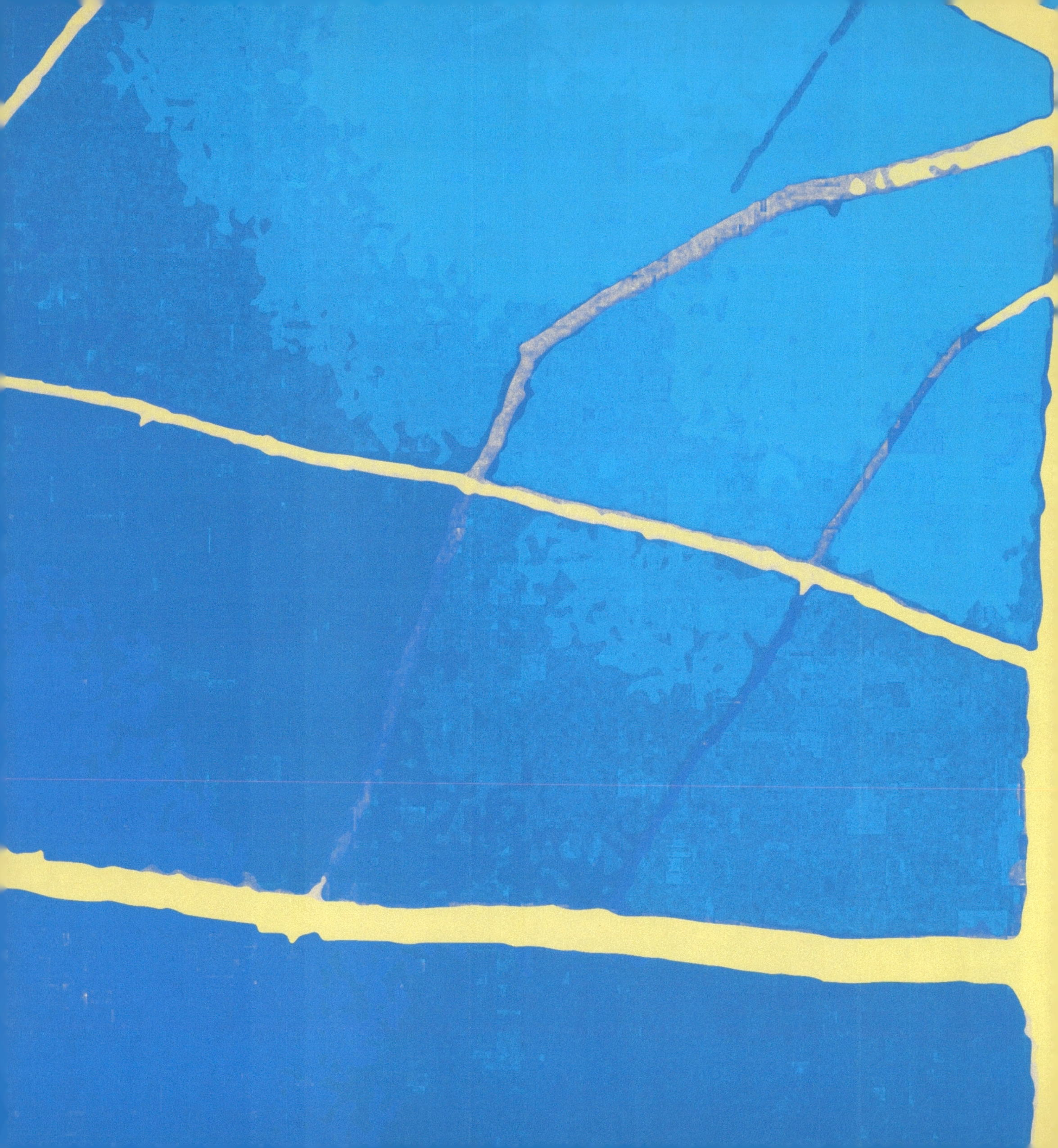

Everything we
don’t want to lose—

In memory.

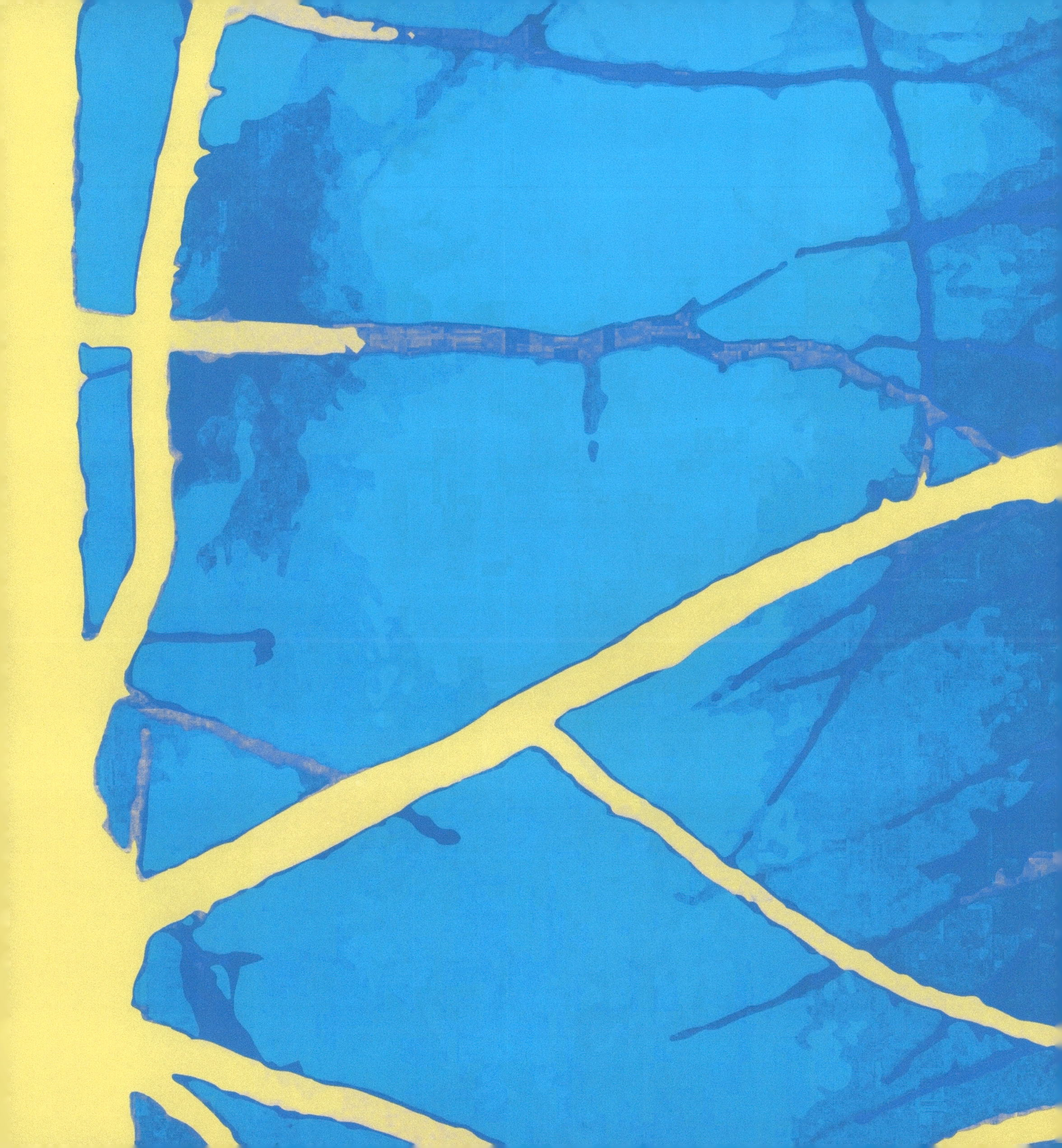

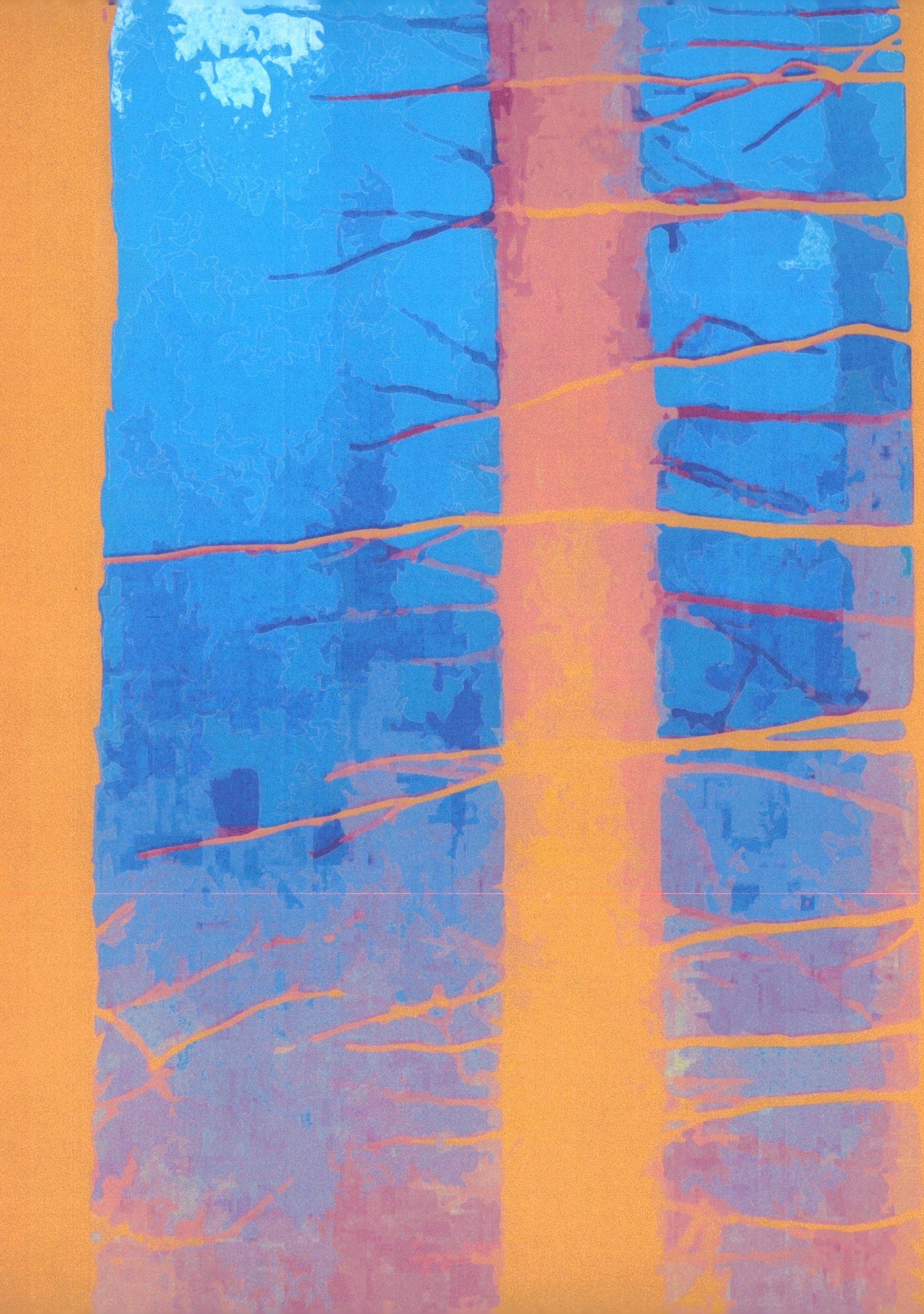

If heaven exists,
I hope it's like this—

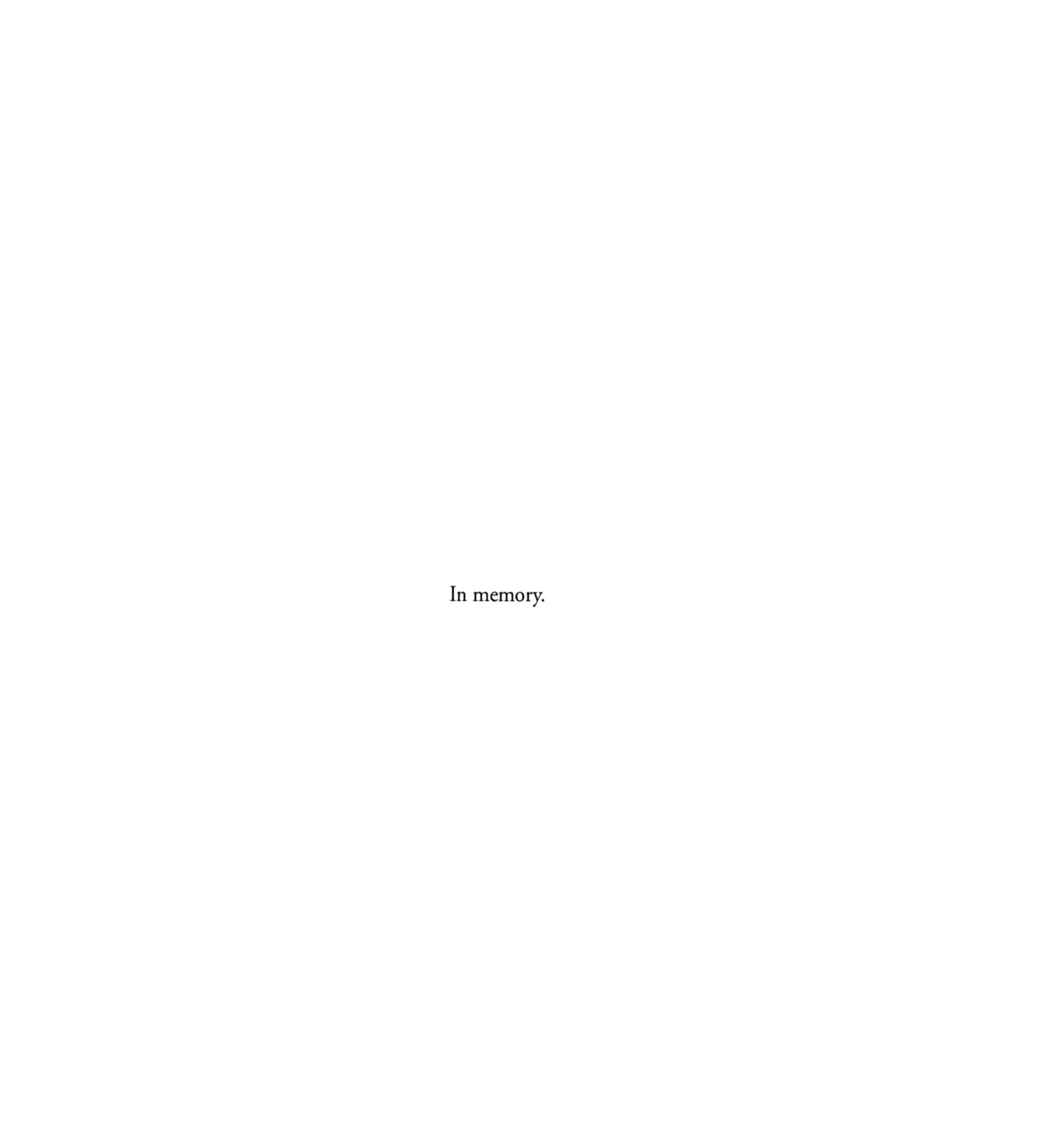
In memory.

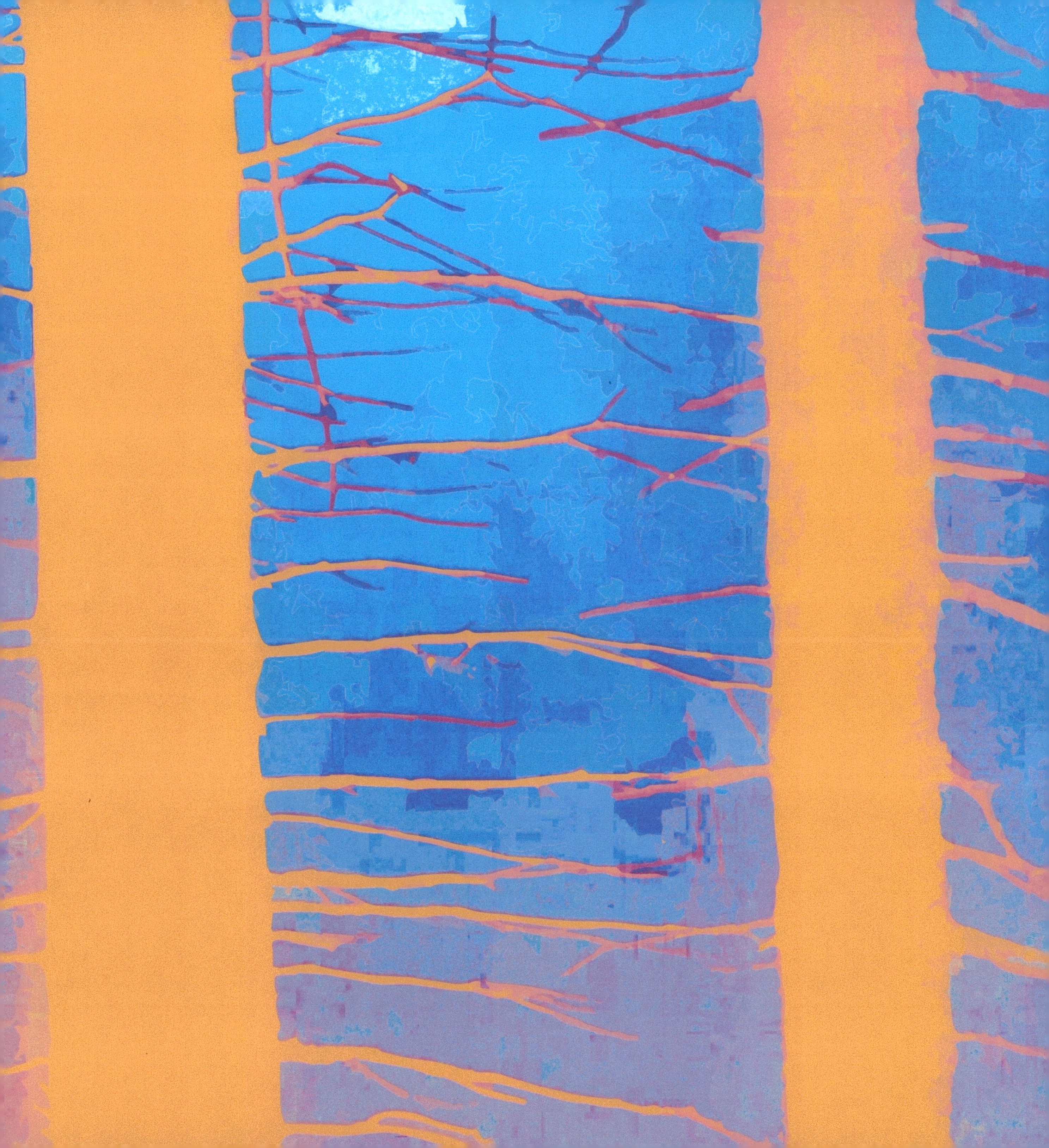

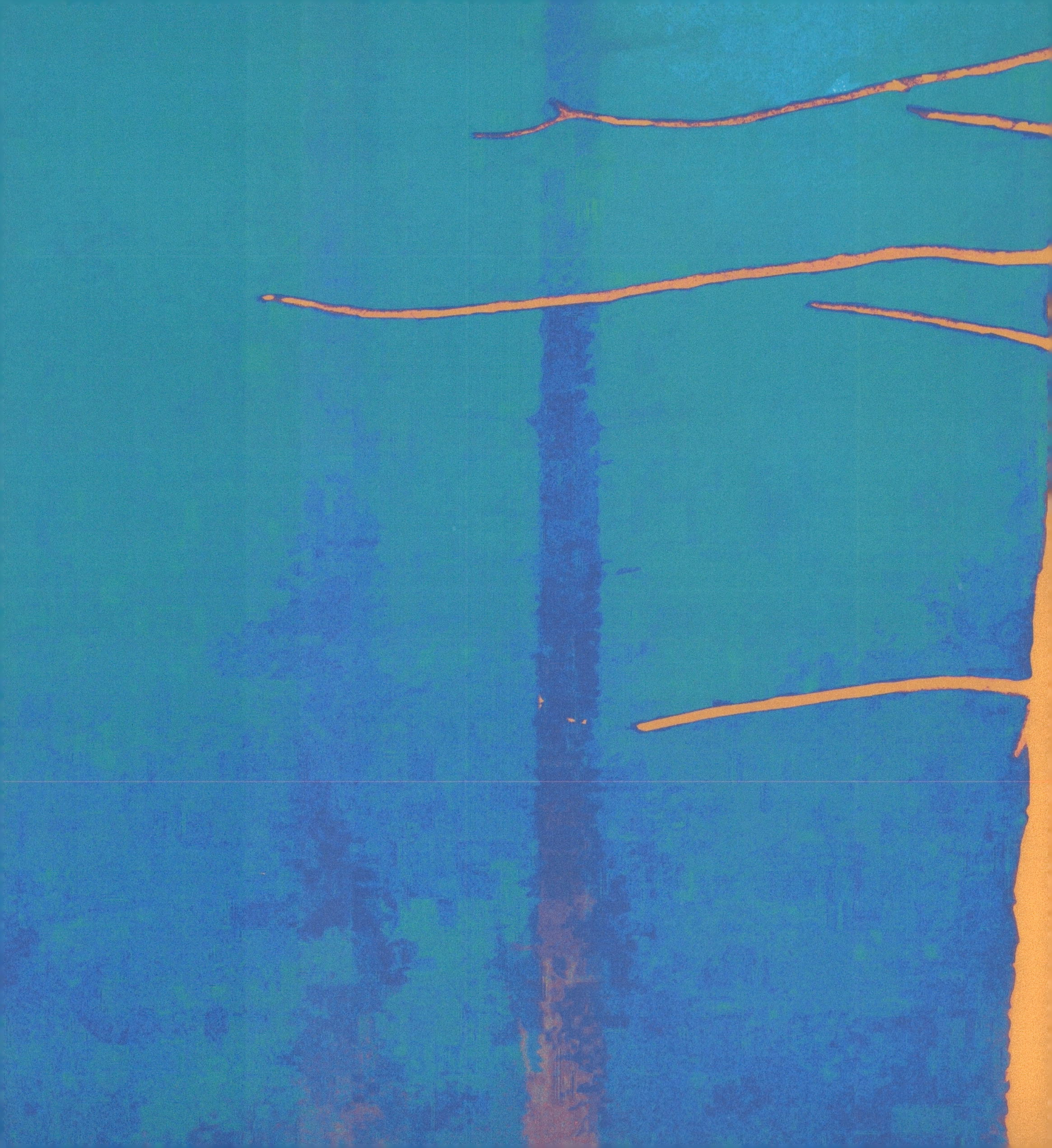

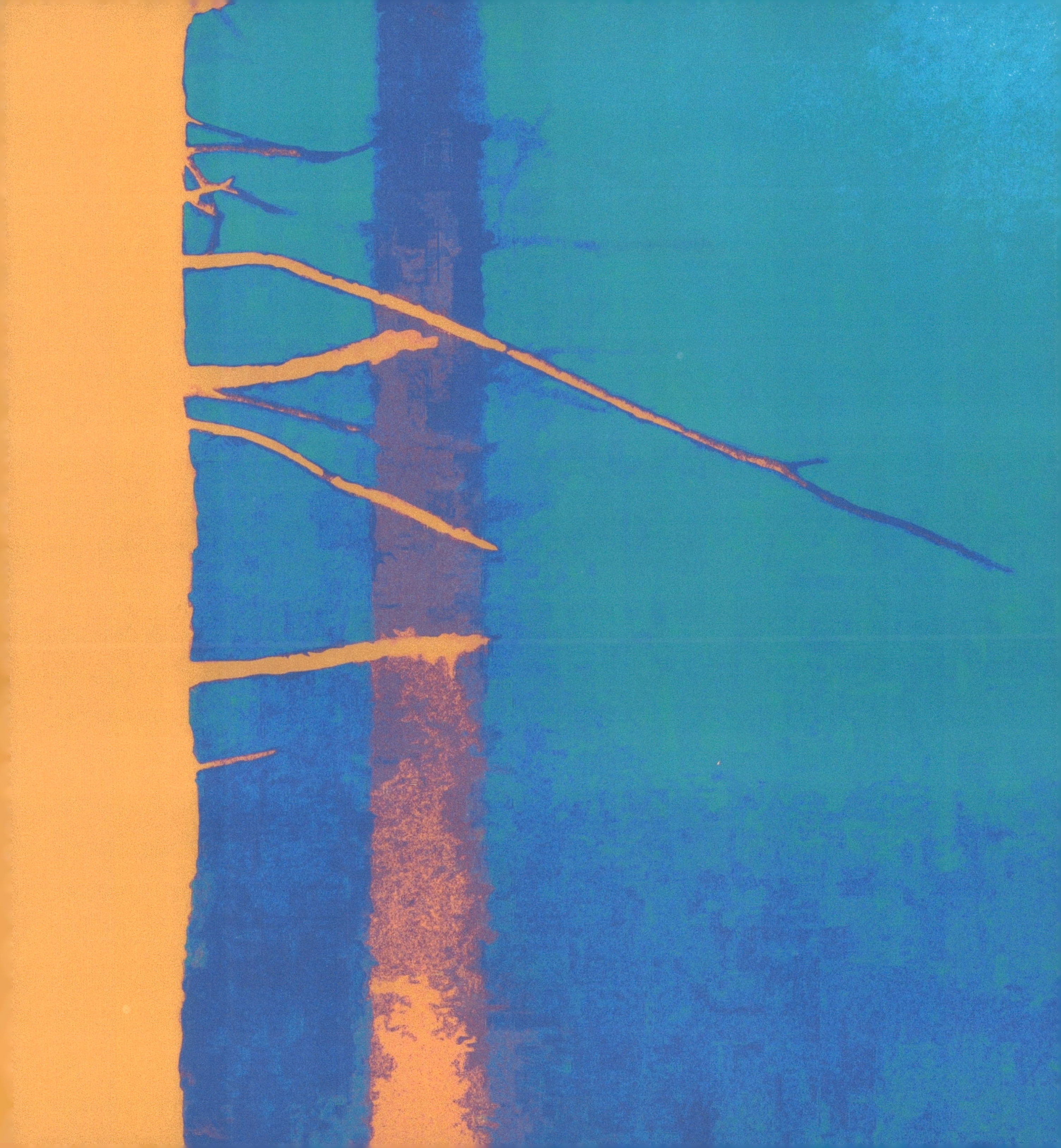

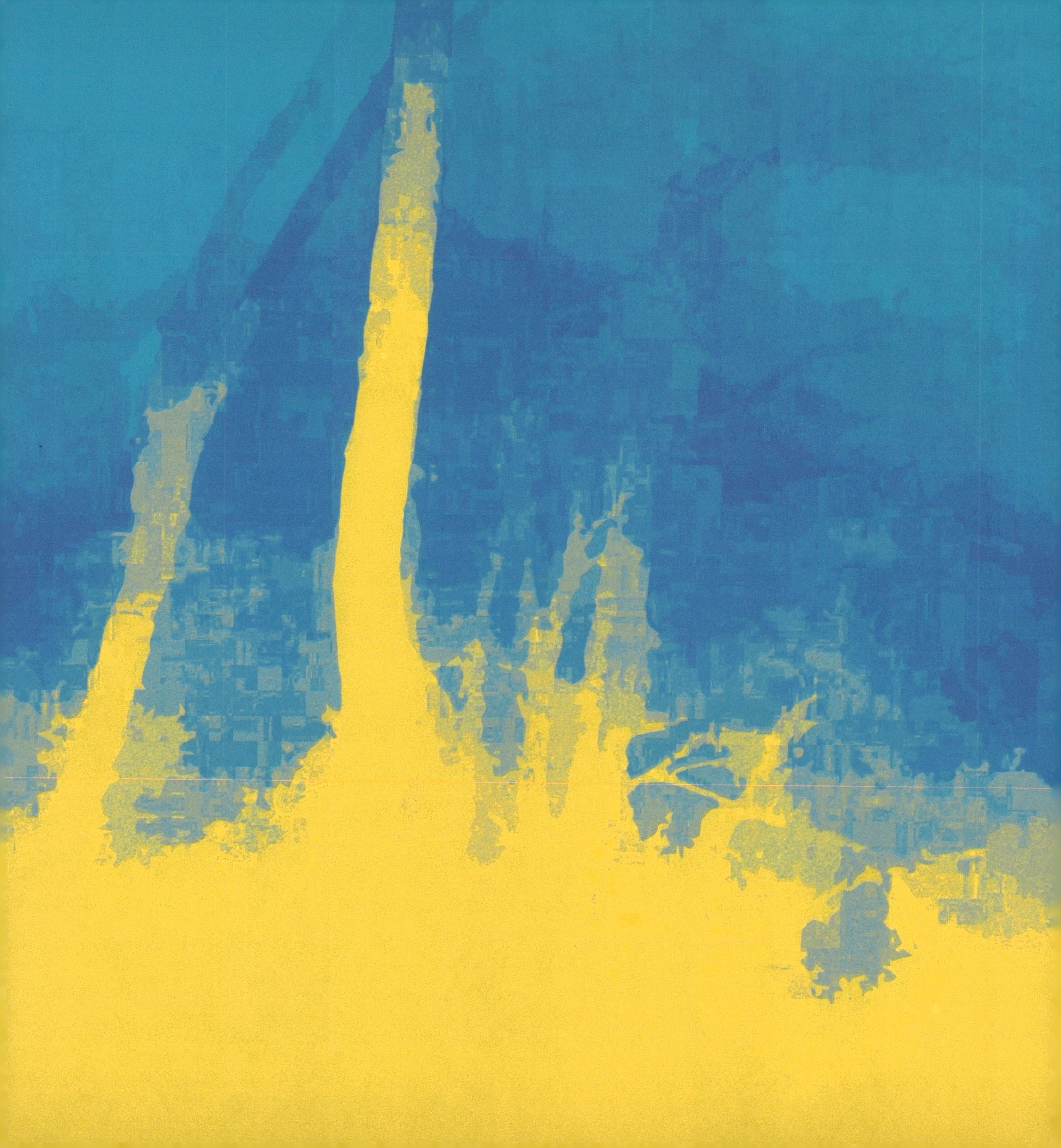

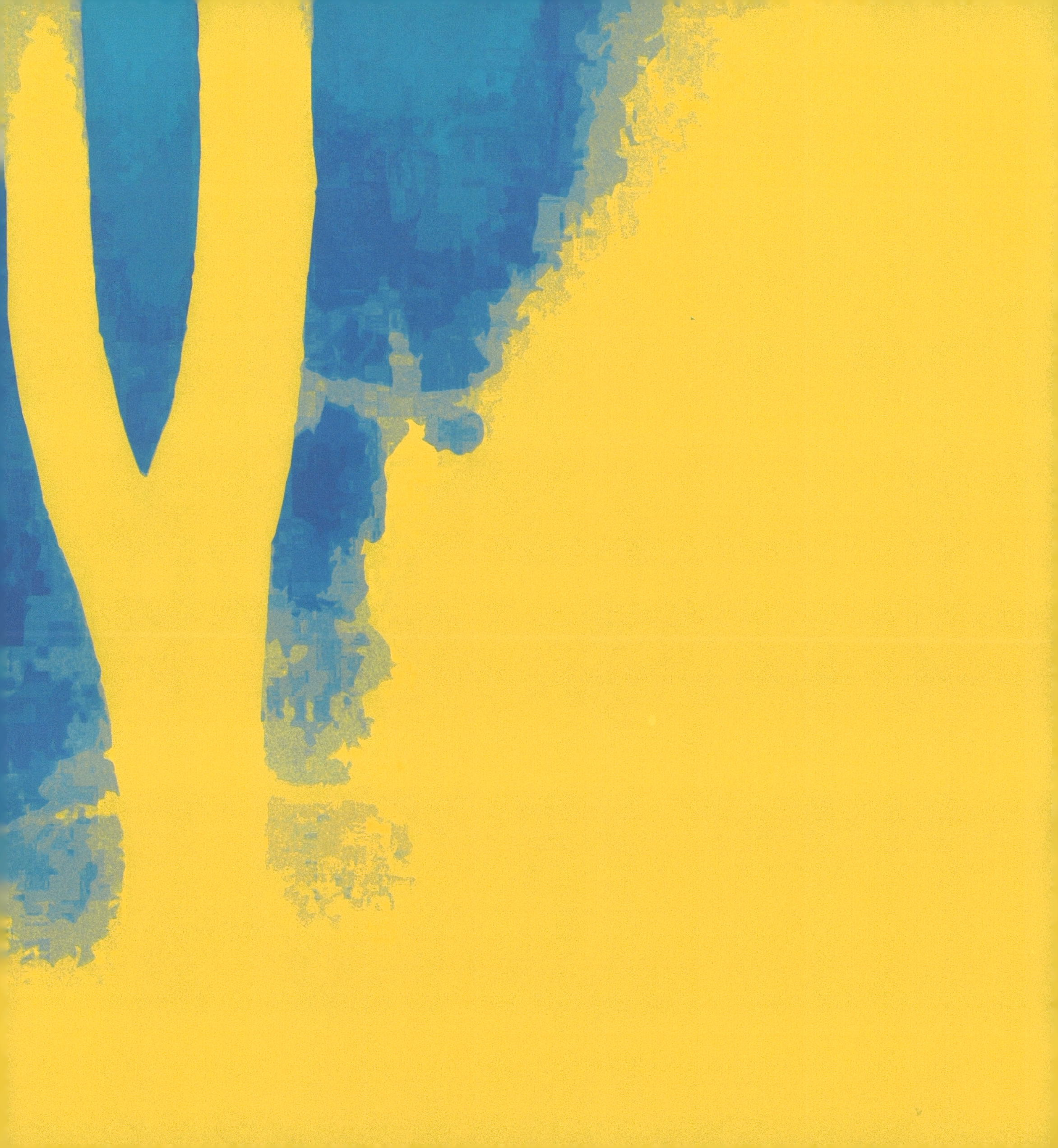

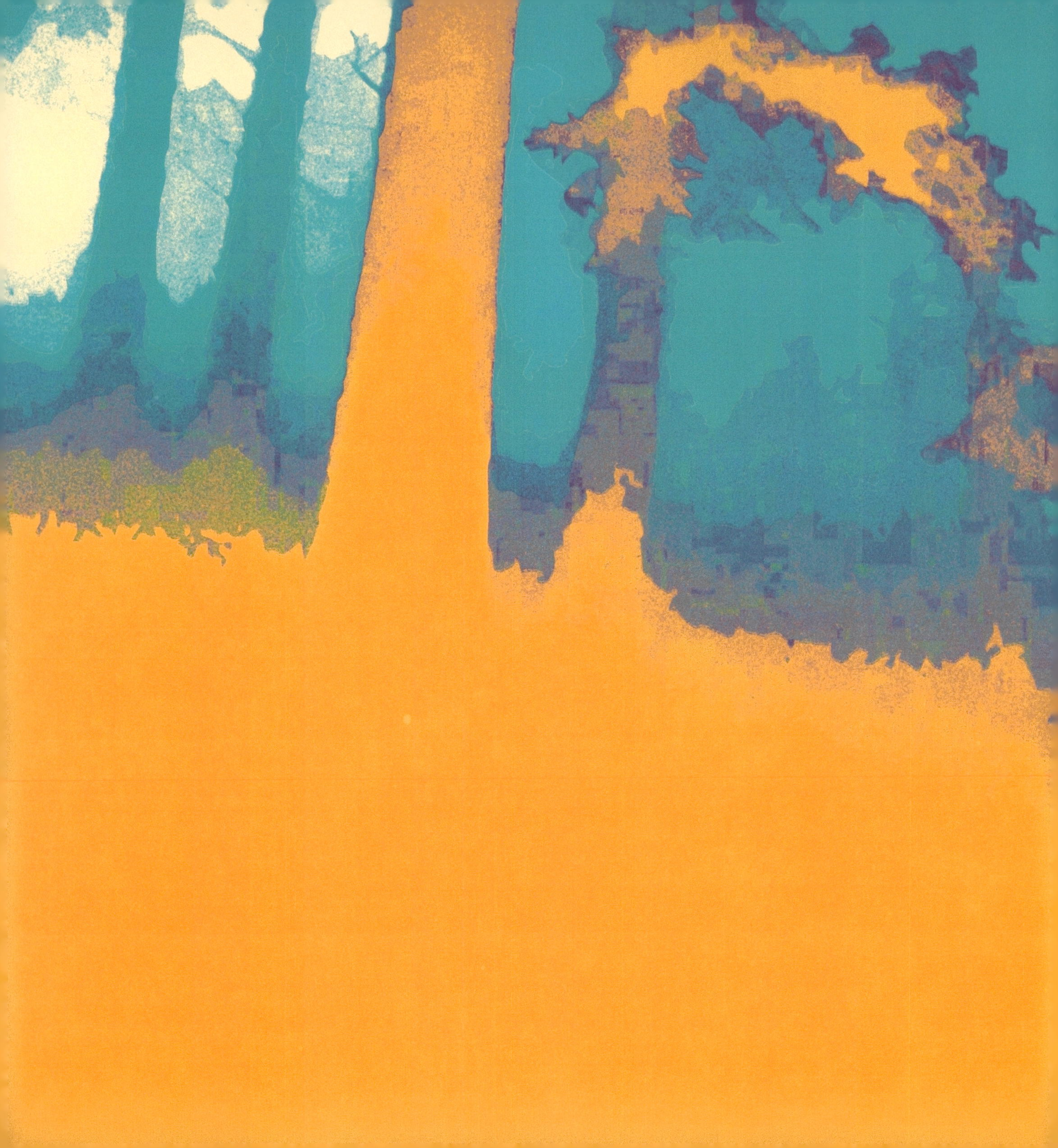

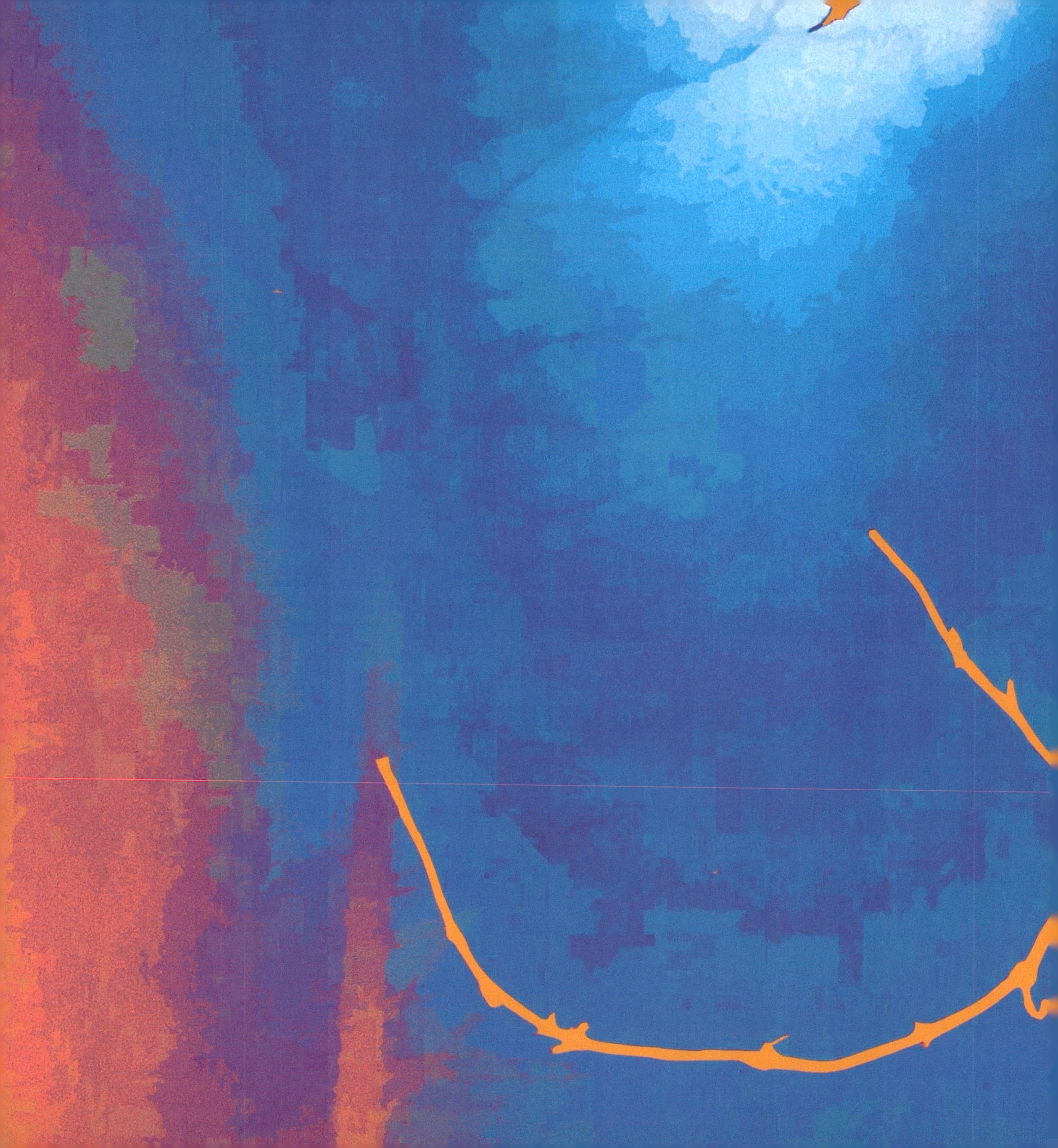

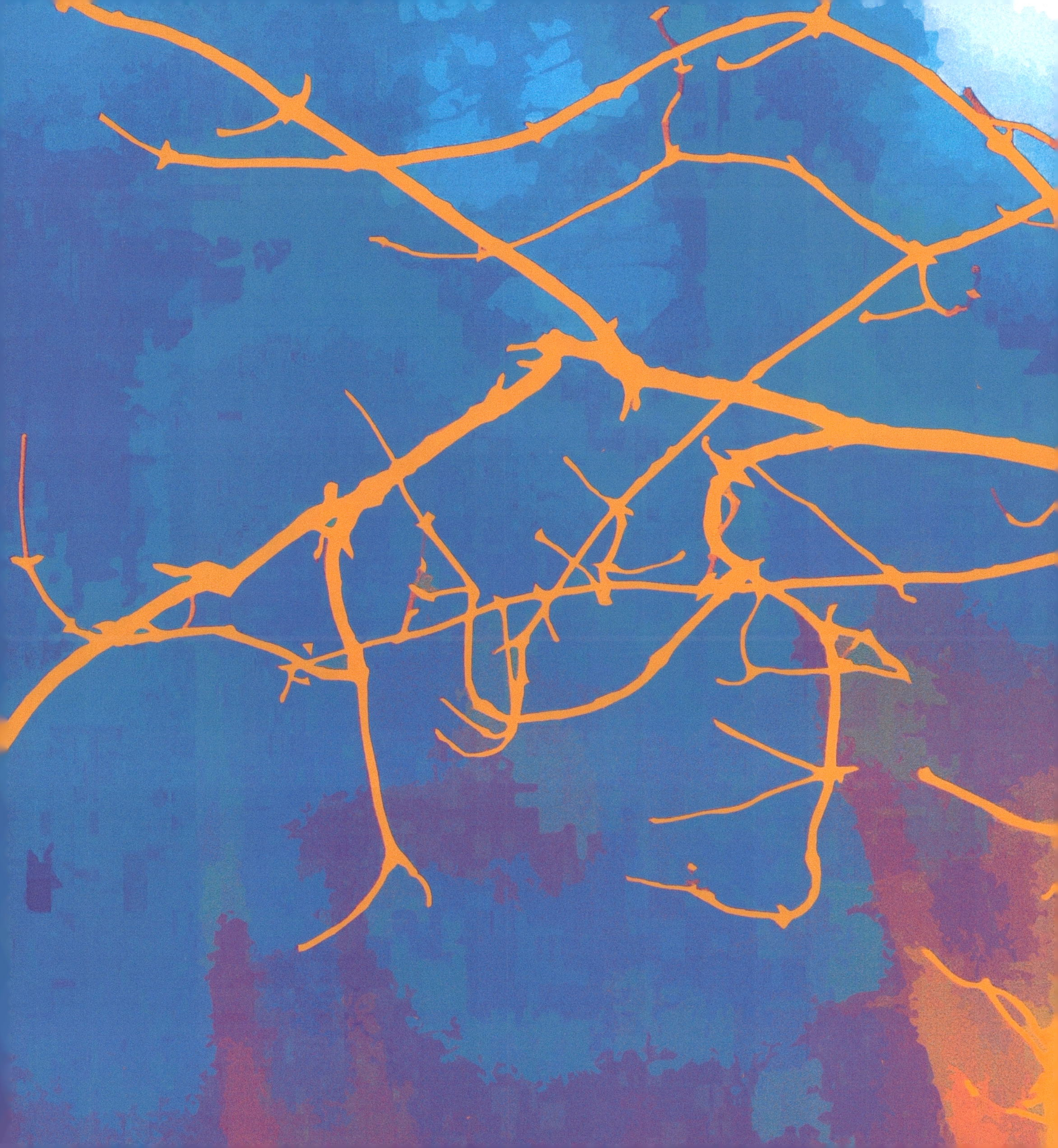

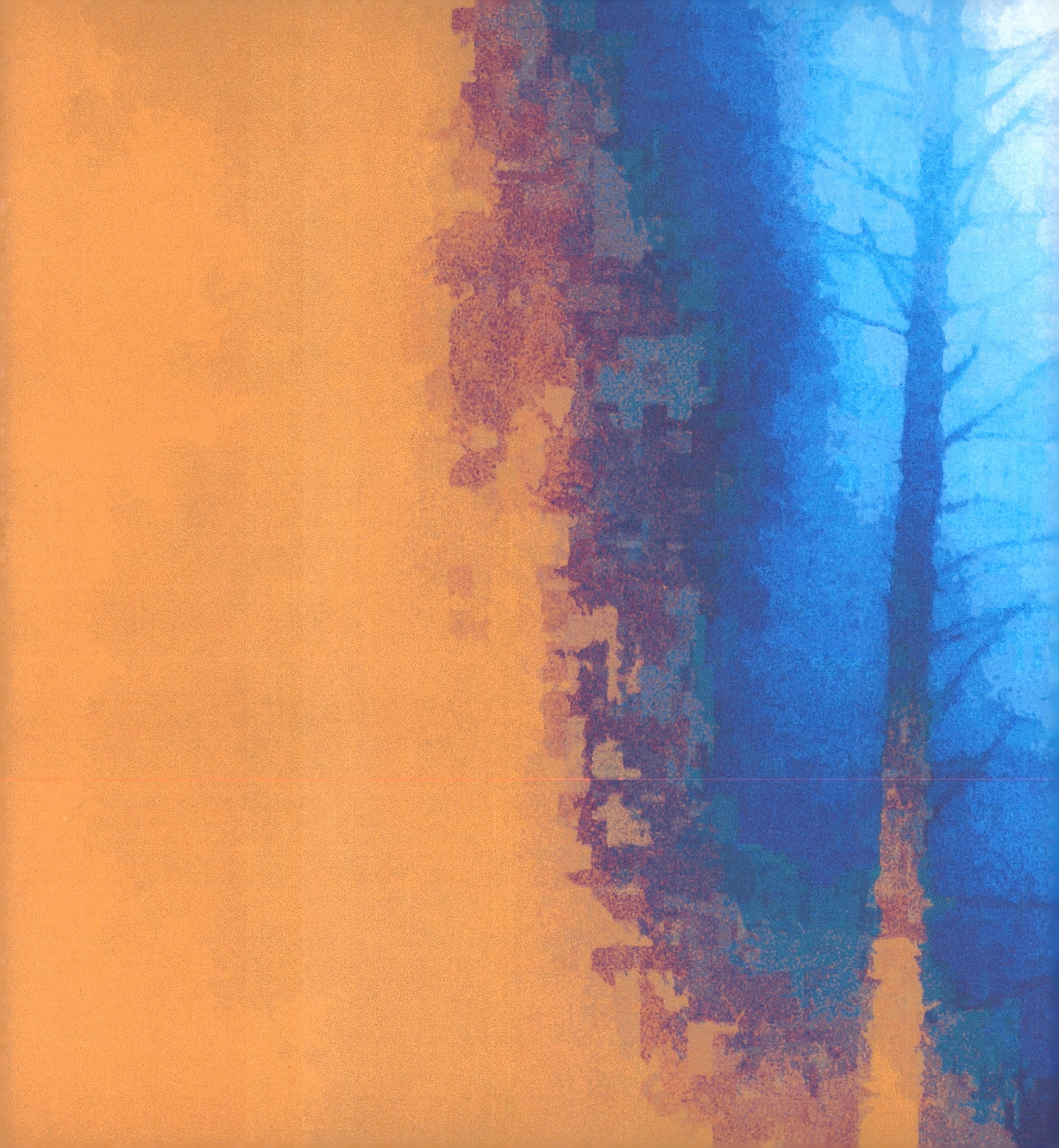

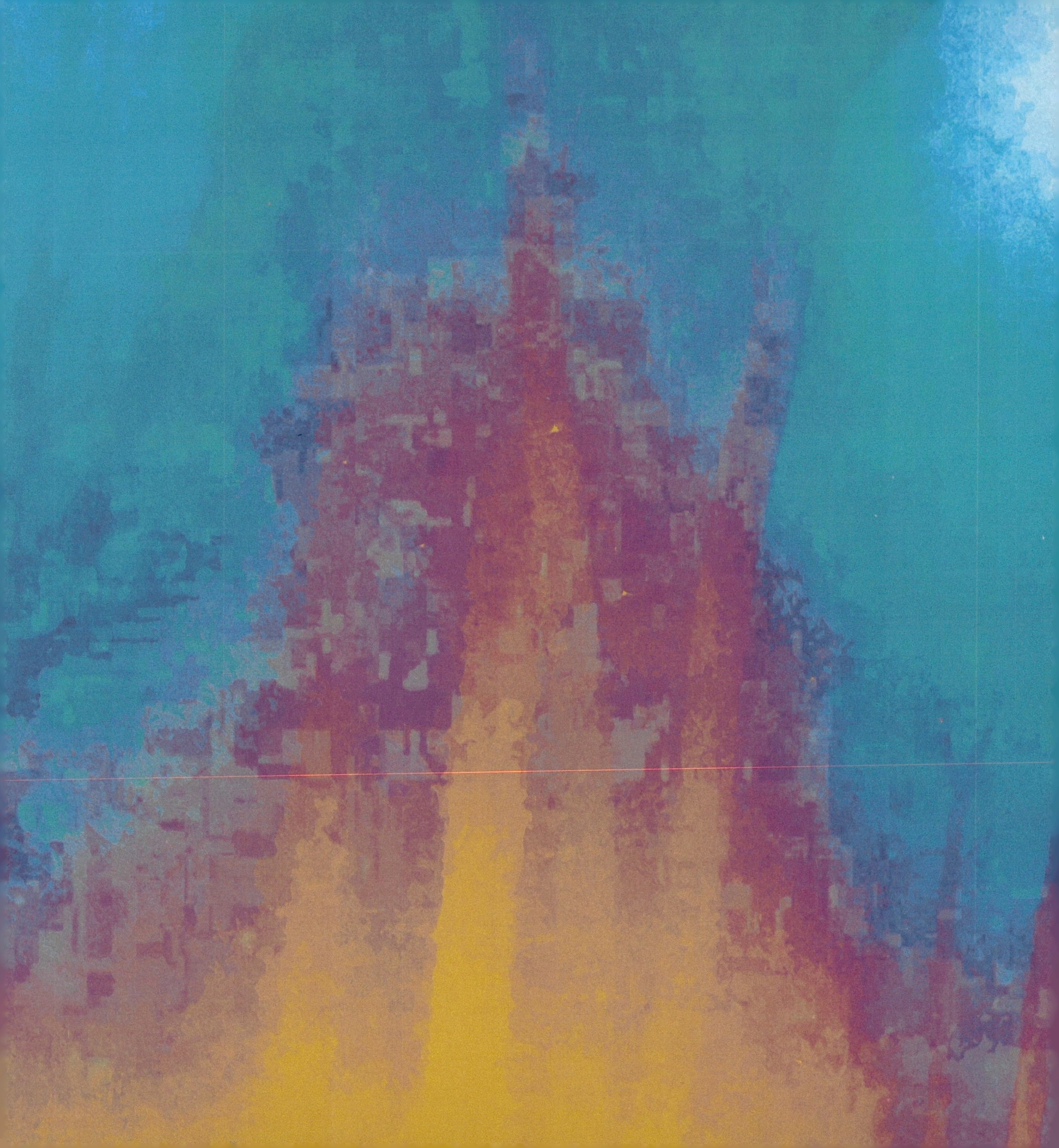

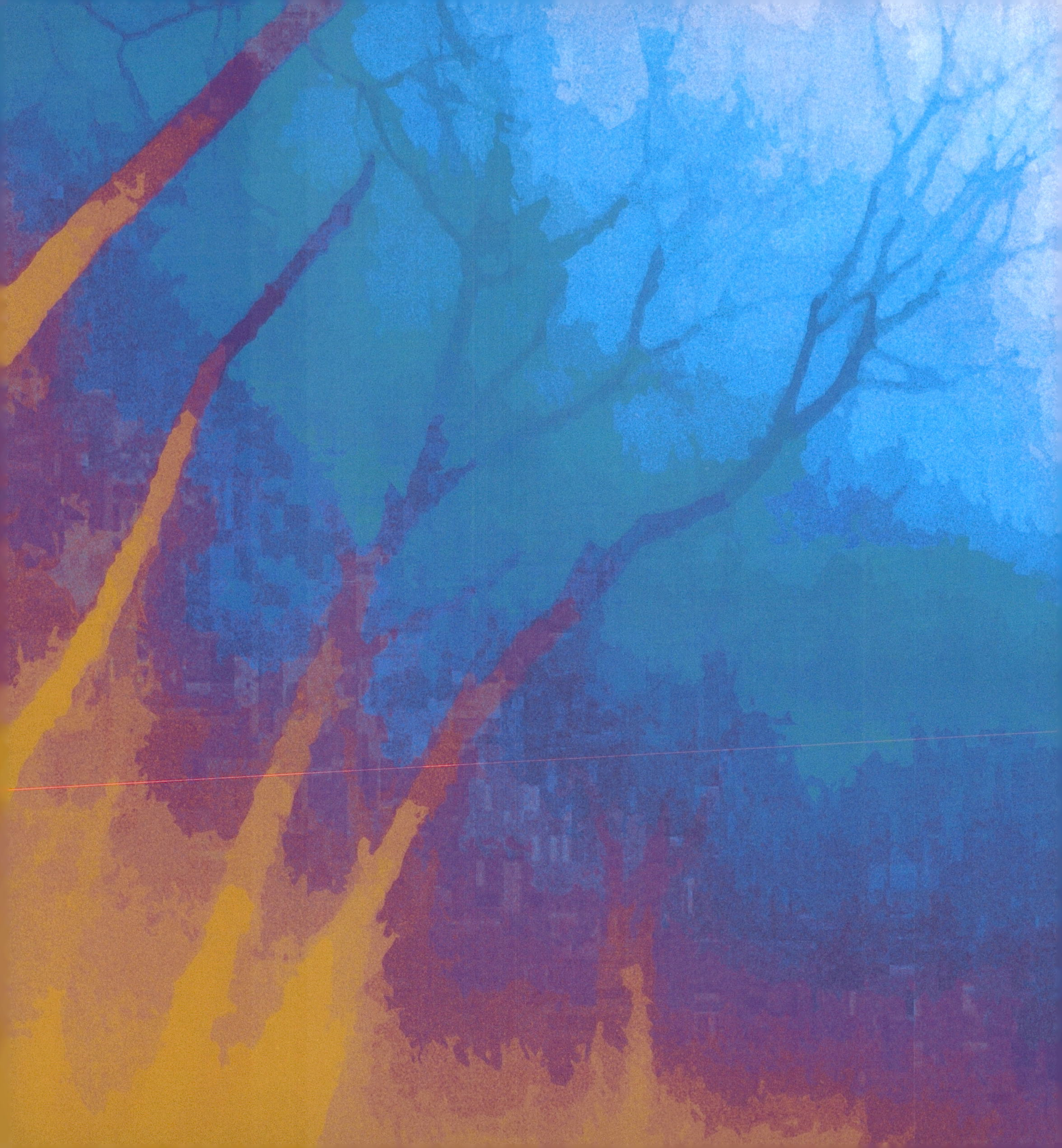

You are the clouds
running on the fields—

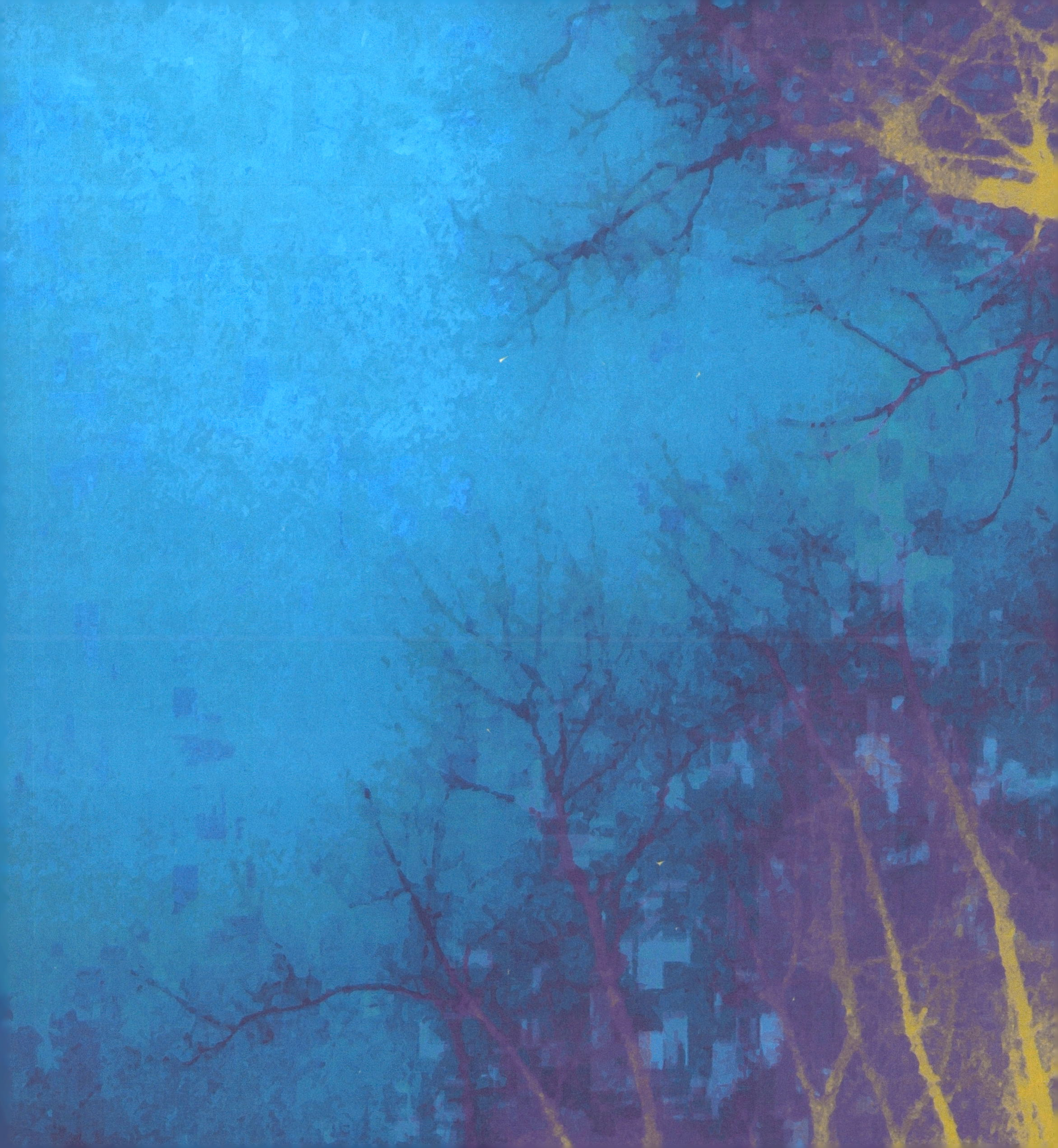

I see you—

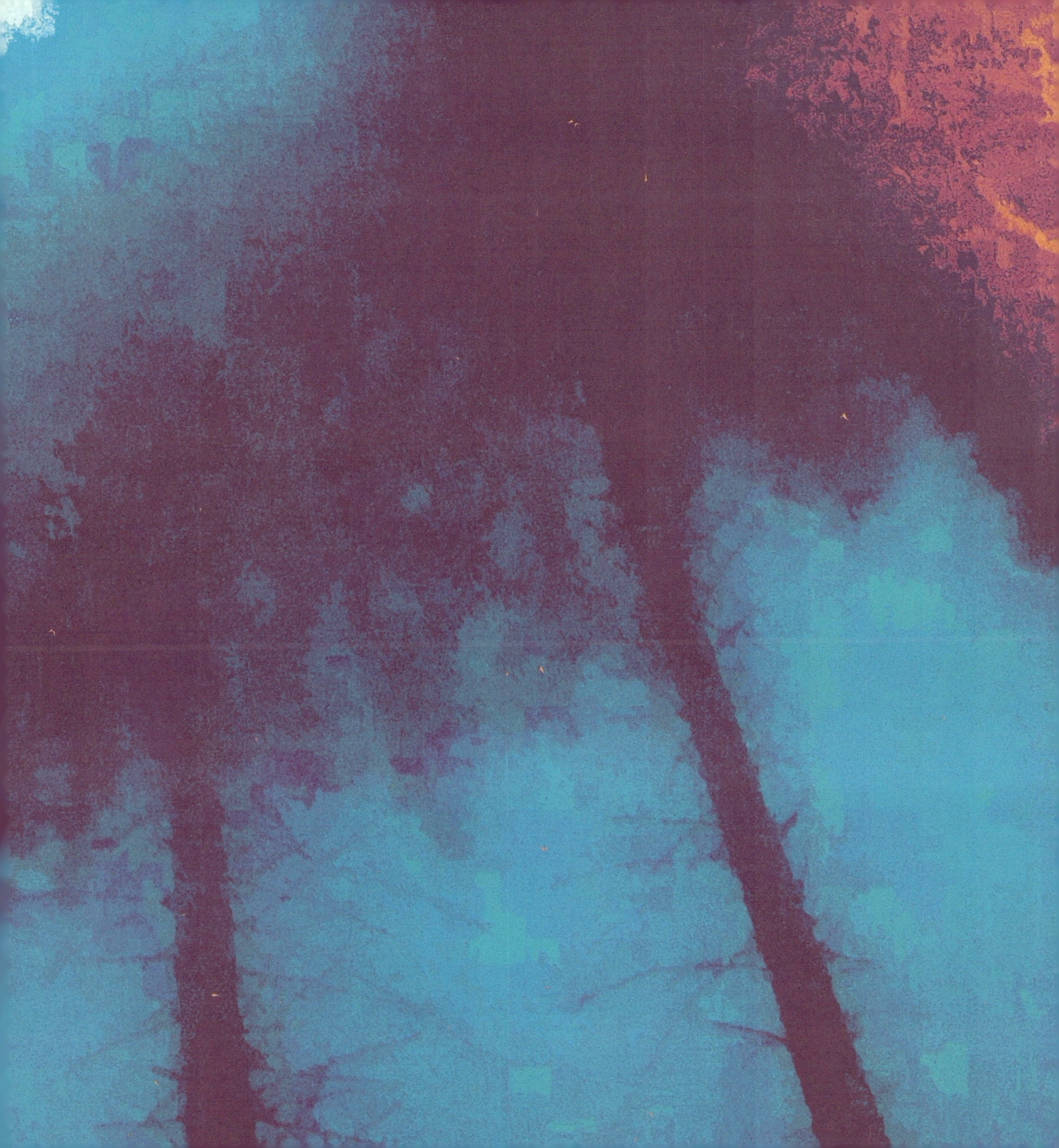

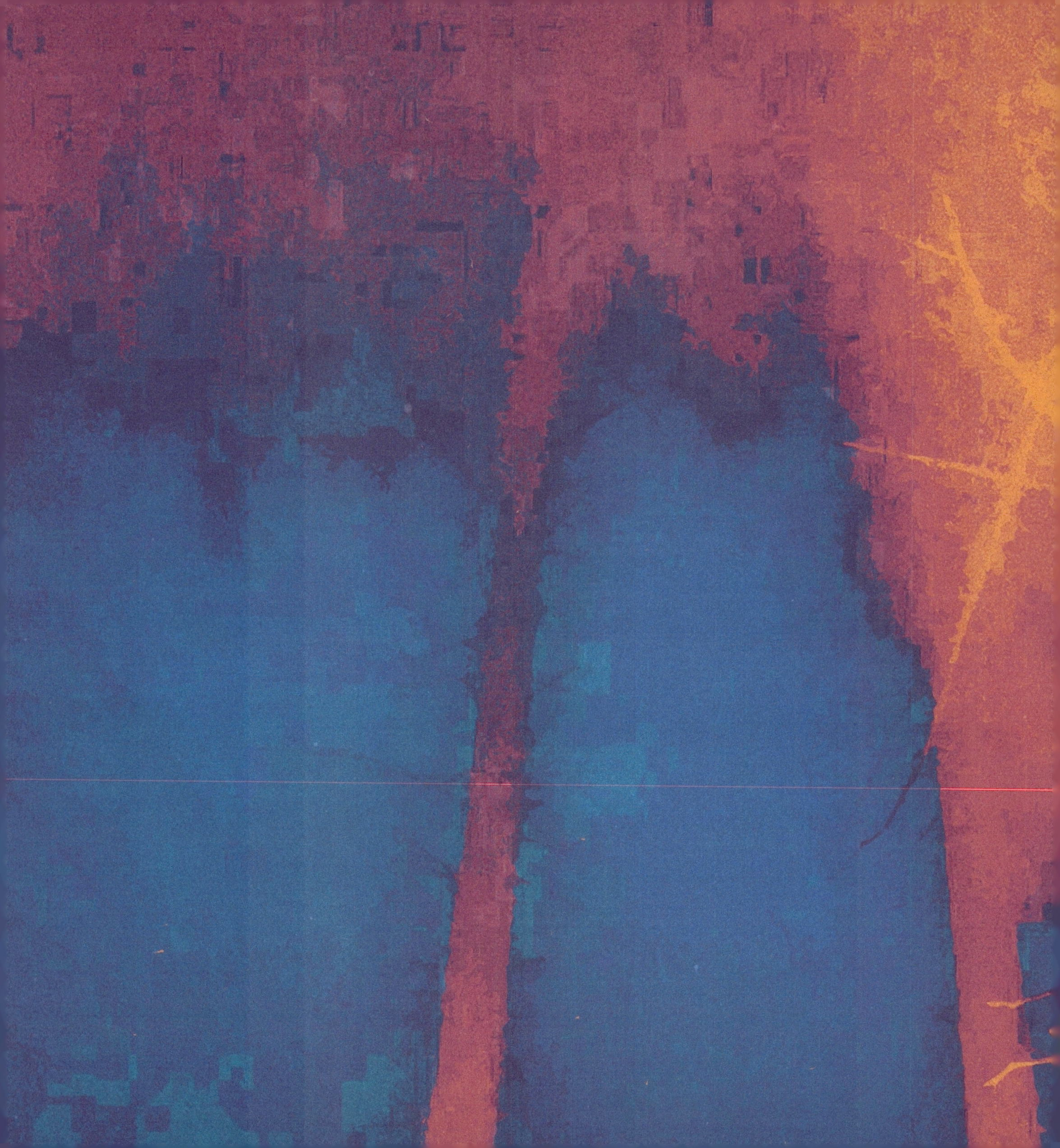

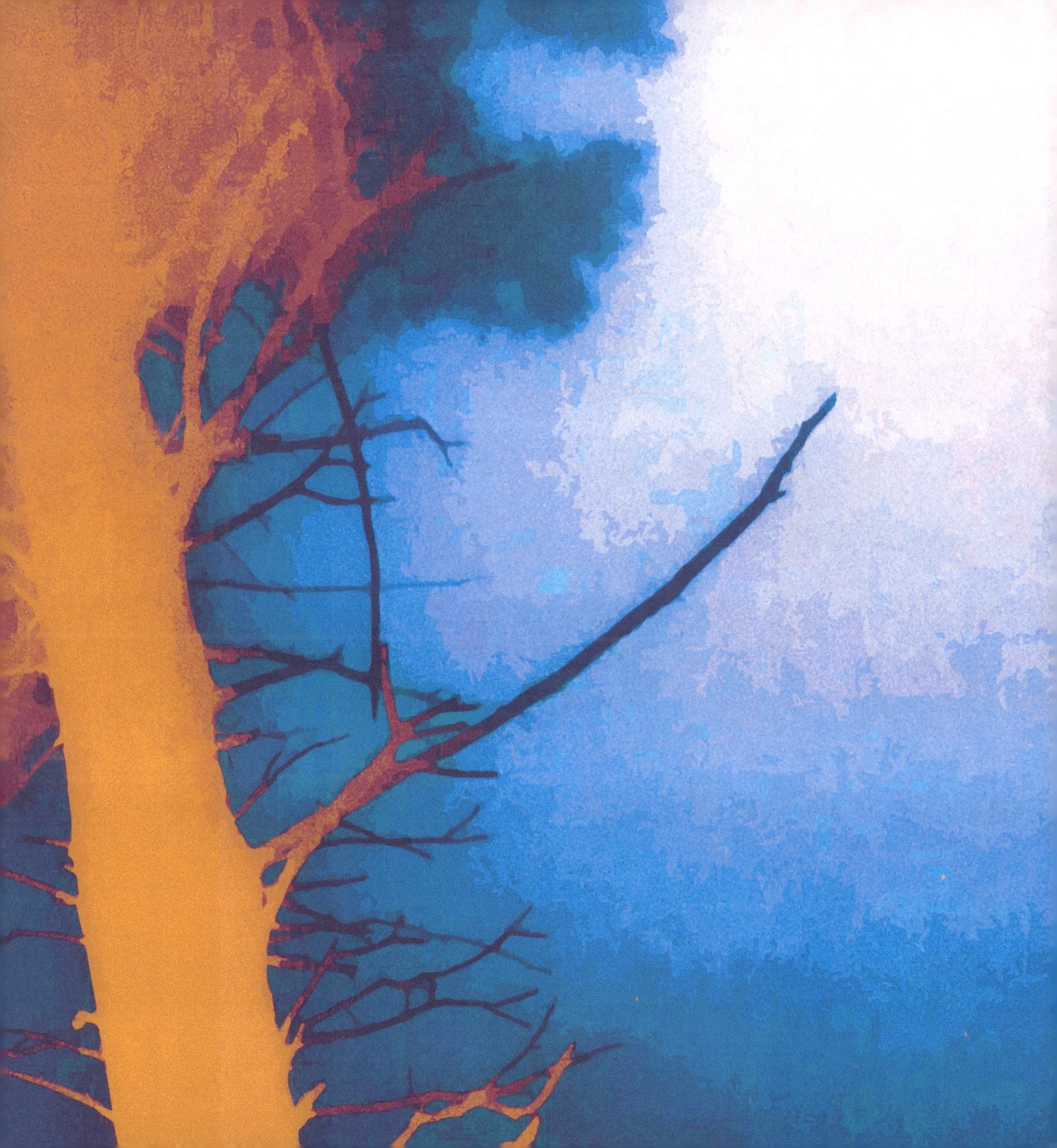

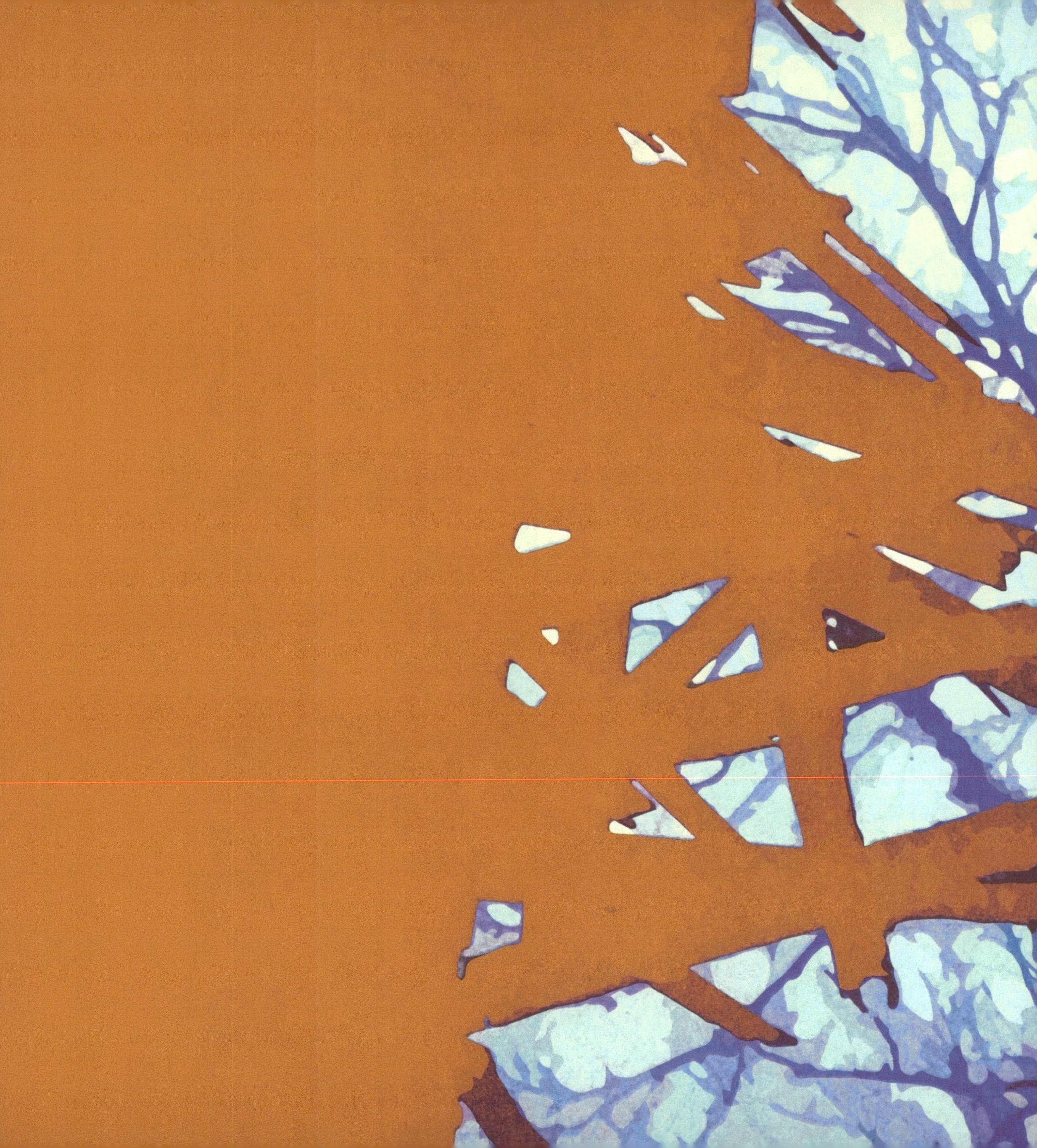

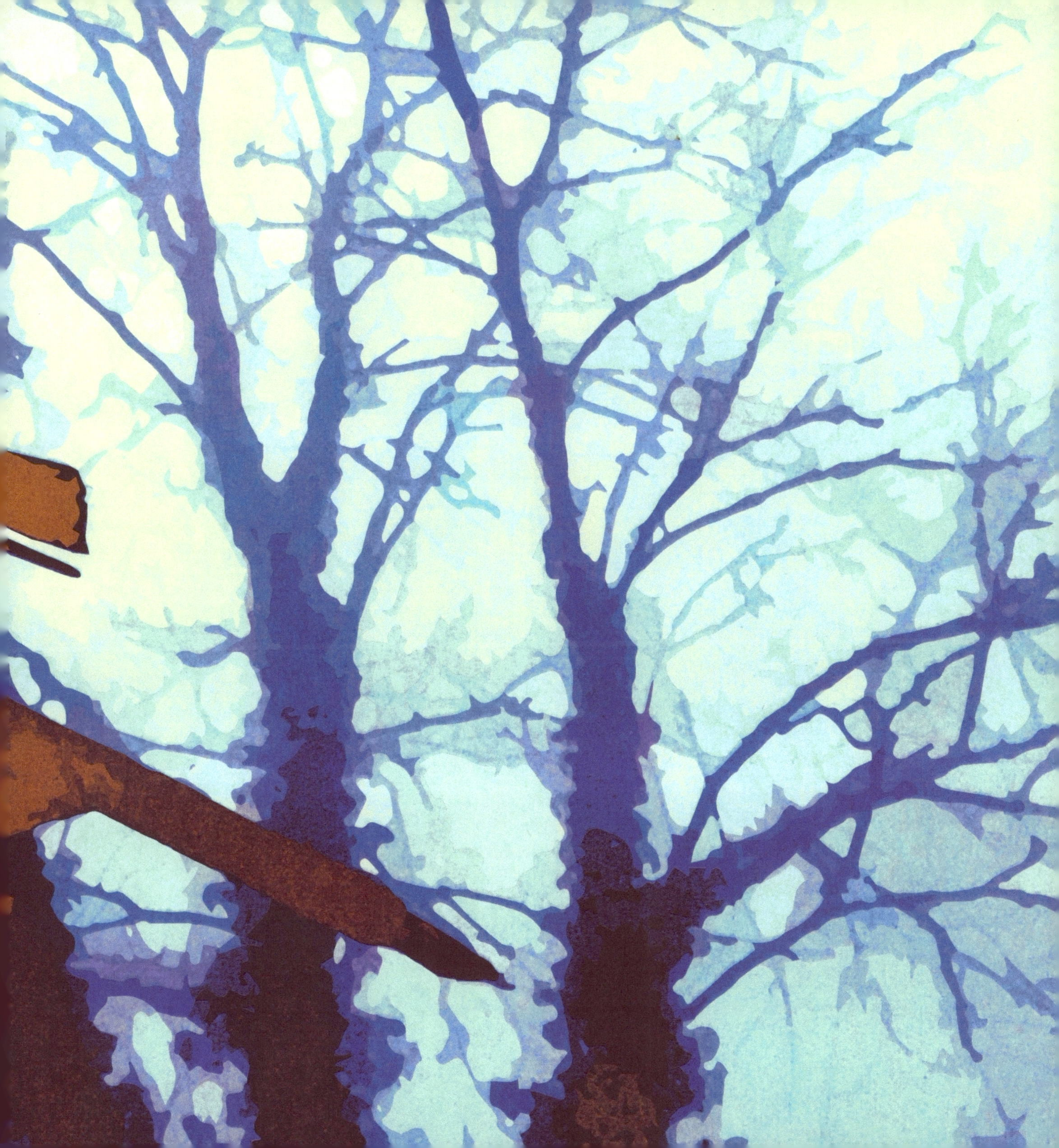

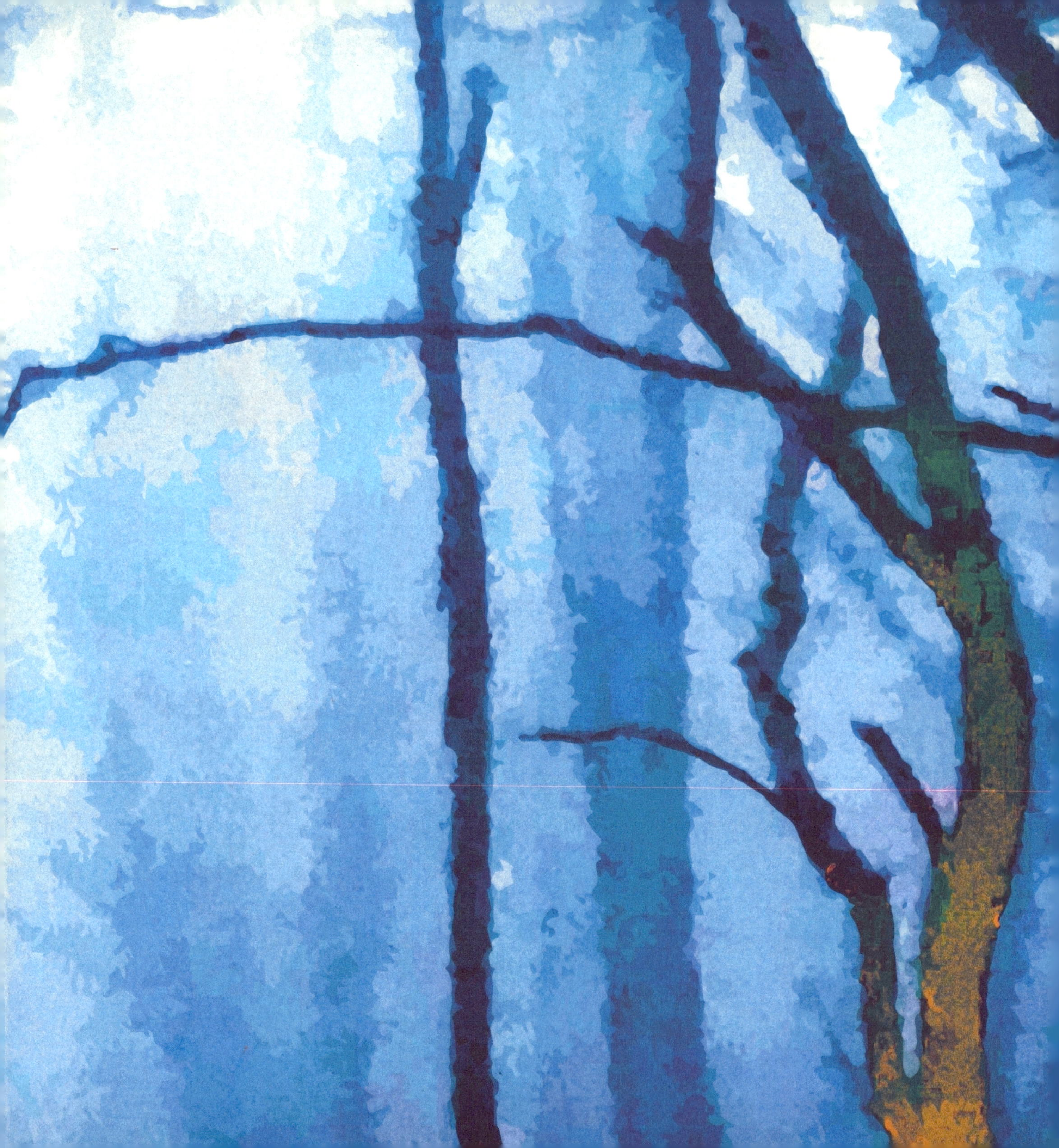

Beyond, further,
beyond me—

In memory.

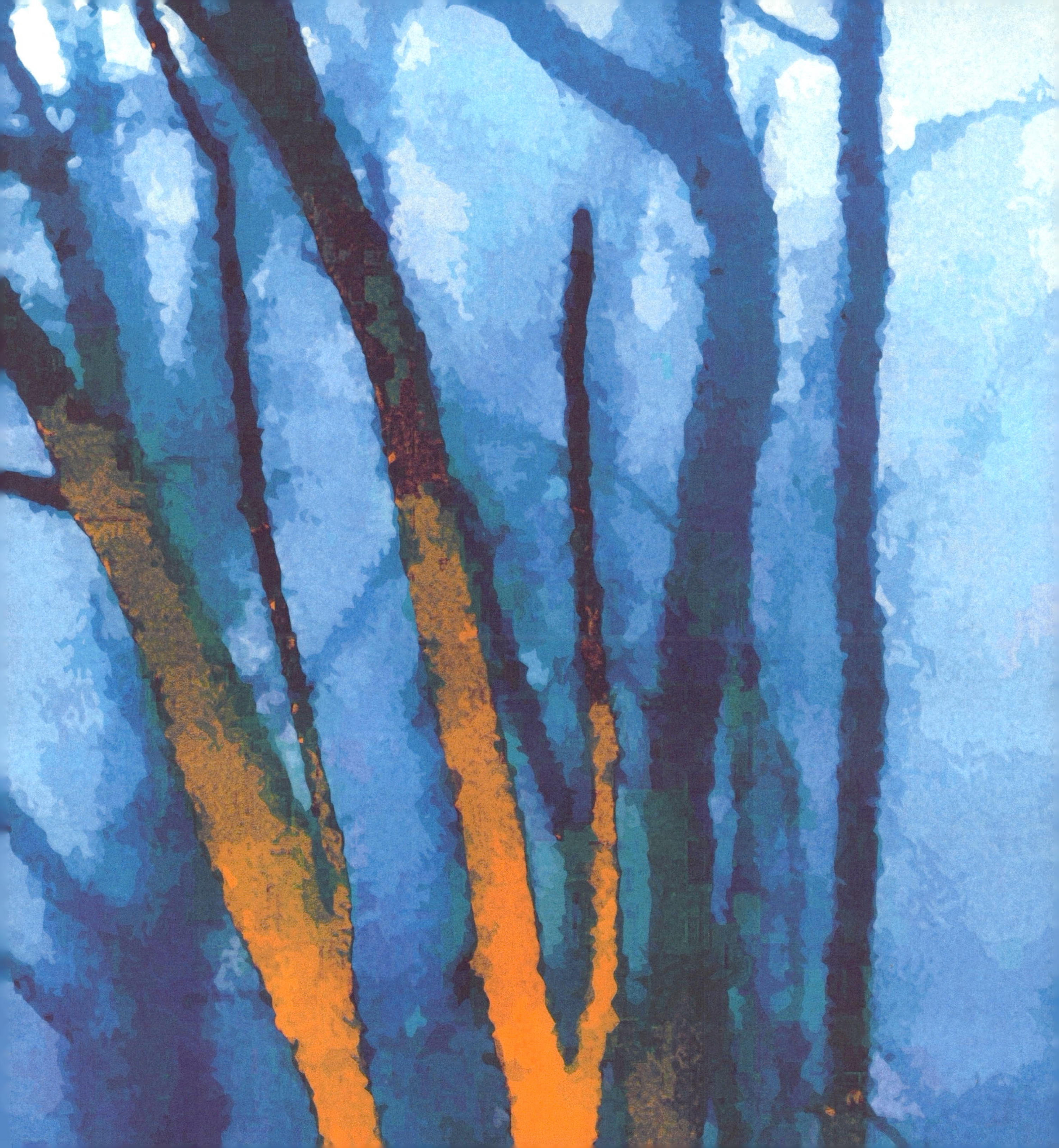

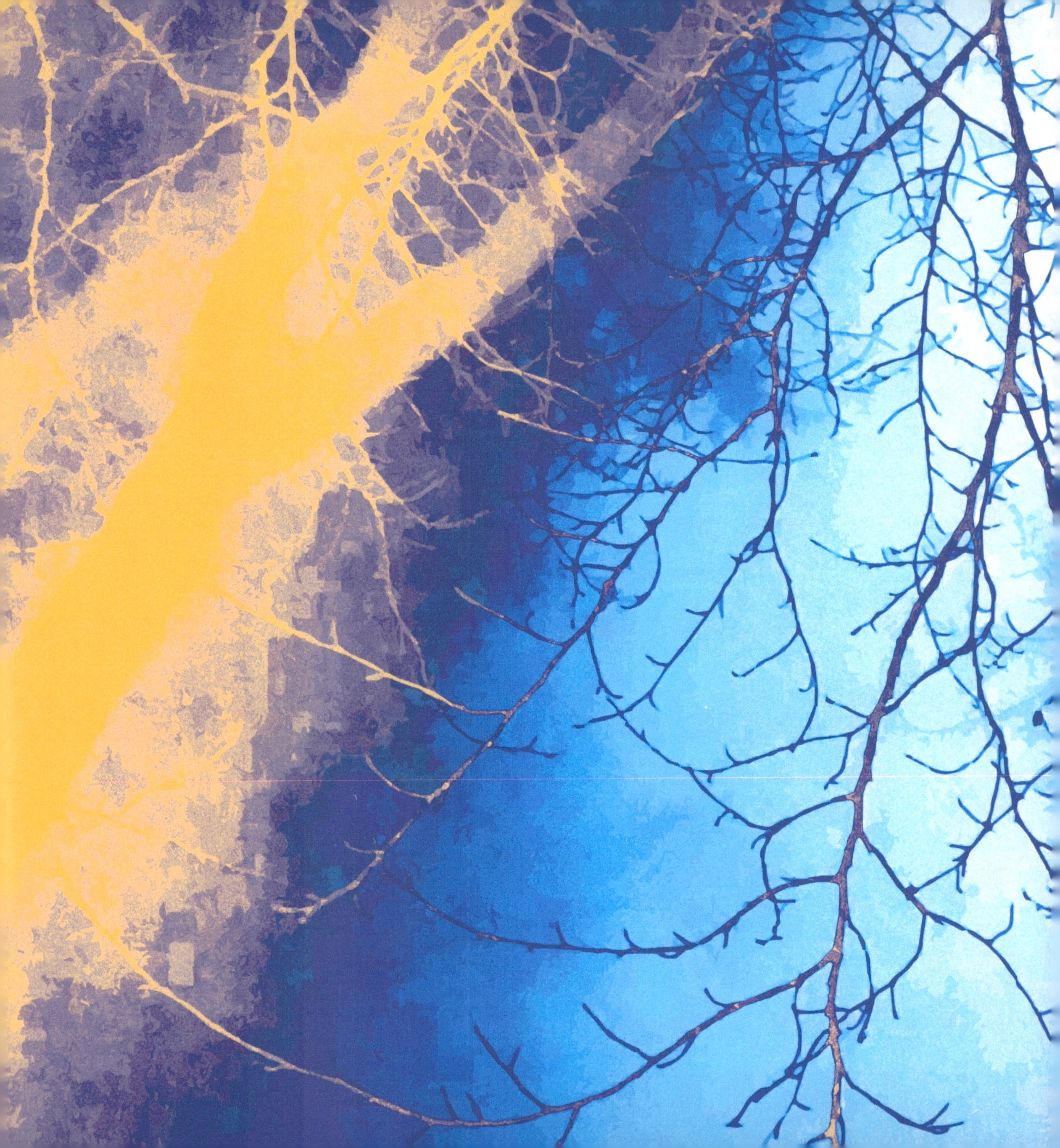

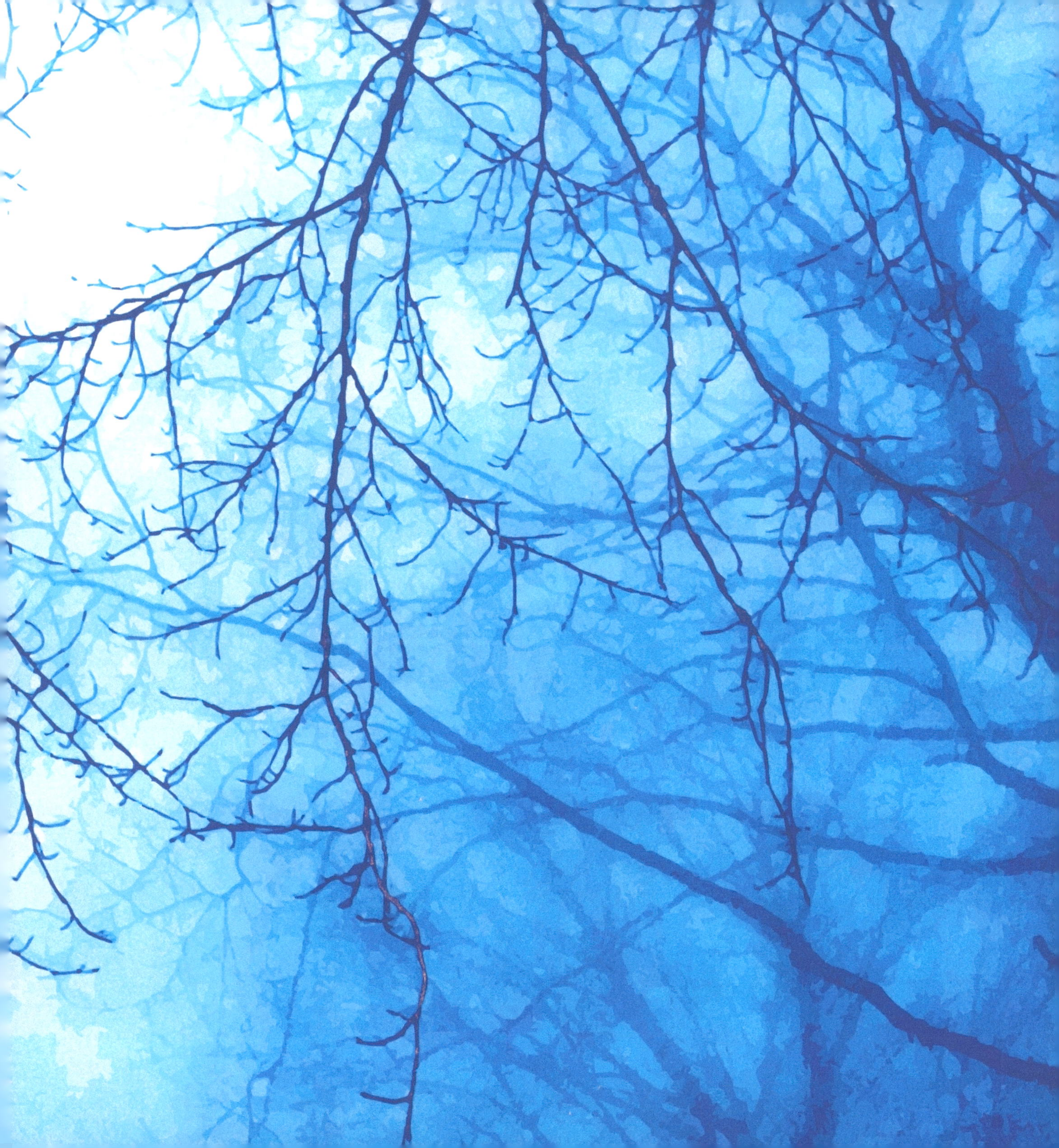

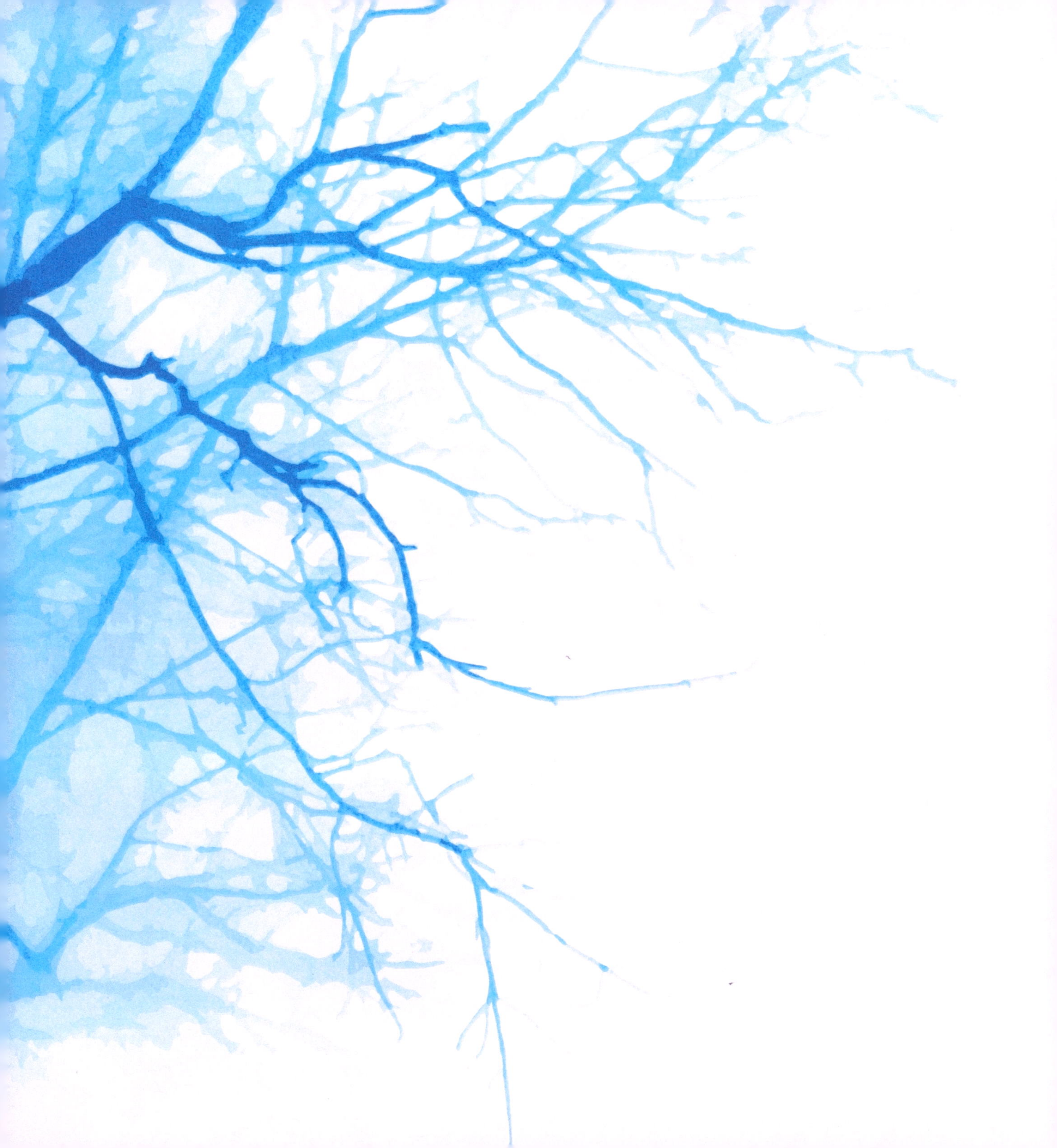

At the end of the world,
we will see our dreams come true.
There's always hope, they say:
build something beautiful
around your void.

But the void *is* the beauty:
love without end,
that comes and goes;
signs of it everywhere,
at the bottom of my soul.
Here, nestled,
God's grammar:

Everything that counts,

In memory.

Everything we don't want to lose,

In memory.

If heaven exists, I hope it's like this,

In memory.

You are the clouds
running on the fields.
I see you. Beyond, further,
beyond me.

In memory.

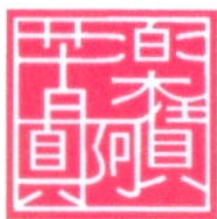

GADFLY
www.gadflyeditions.com

www.ingramcontent.com/pod-product-compliance
Lightning Source LLC
LaVergne TN
LVHW071631100826
845154LV00008BA/134
* 9 7 8 0 9 9 2 8 0 6 0 7 1 *